L. cordua

THE LIBRARY OF HISTORY AND DOCTRINE

THE EMPEROR THEODOSIUS
AND THE
ESTABLISHMENT OF CHRISTIANITY

THE LIBRARY OF HISTORY AND DOCTRINE

The aim of this international Library is to enable scholars to answer questions about the development of the Christian tradition which are important for an understanding of Christianity today.

THE
EMPEROR THEODOSIUS
AND THE ESTABLISHMENT
OF CHRISTIANITY

N. Q. KING

*Professor of Divinity
and Fellow of Akuafo Hall
in the University College of Ghana*

Philadelphia
The Westminster Press

PRINTED IN GREAT BRITAIN

To
The Department of Divinity
in the University College of Ghana

CONTENTS

MAP
The Episcopal Sees known to have been represented at the
Second Oecumenical Council, Constantinople, A.D. 381

PREFACE

THIS IS a small epitaph to the 'Constantine, Theodosius and all that' era. As we stand here with our hats in our hands, rejoicing perhaps as we think of the chains which have been struck off, no one could blame some of us for hankering once again after those fetters of gold. Less should we condemn those far-sighted ones who can visualize the new manacles and ham-stringings which are being prepared in some places, or the contemptuous ignoring as irrelevant which most will give us.

These studies in the relationships of those two totalitarian bodies the Church and the State in the late fourth century, were originally prompted by a purely scholarly and antiquarian interest, but as the study proceeded questions more closely relevant to the modern world kept obtruding themselves. Free and vigorous independent States are emerging in Africa and Asia. They have all to make a decision about their official religion. Some have already declared for Islam, some are accepting Communism, some give lip-service to the slogan of religious neutrality, a few may even declare themselves Christian. In each of these countries there are Christian groups who will have to work out their relationship to that great Leviathan, the modern omnipotent State. At one extreme, certain Christian groups will decide to carry their religion actively into party politics and will attempt to get control of the government. At the other, certain groups will refuse to have anything to do with what they consider this beast from the abyss. These new nations and the Muslim, Buddhist, Christian or Communist groups within them can learn from the fourth-century Roman settlement what happens to a religion when it takes over or is taken over by the State and what happens to the State. He who rides on the back of a tiger will never dismount, but in the religion/state partnership, which is the tiger?

The decision about what attitude Church and State should adopt towards one another has grown no easier, but a study of what was done before raises fundamental questions which may throw light on the contemporary debate. In a benevolent State, where does co-operation with the government become dangerous for both partners? If the Church is to play its full part, for instance in education, can it do without the tremendous technical and financial resources which the State can so easily provide, but is the risk of having to be subservient for fear of losing subsidies too great? At which point does the Church stop being a sob-sister, who shrieks when the smallest misdemeanour is committed by the State, and add her voice to the congratulatory chorus? In a State which is establishing an orthodoxy, be it religious, political or economic, where does resistance begin or should there be no resistance? What of the duty to resist evil, if only for the good of the wrong-doer? Or again, is the best relationship between Church and State a dual one, each going its own way: is such a dualism possible when neither Church nor State will concede that it is not all-embracing? In dealing with groups all of which claim to be orthodox is there an alternative to the Theodosian way, other than the indifference of toleration?

The Roman Empire of Arcadius and Honorius was very different from that of Aurelian and the young Diocletian. The change in its character was only surpassed by the change which had overtaken the Church during the fourth century. Ecclesiastical history is to the Church as memory is to man. With its aid remembrance of past events can be summoned to serve in present difficulties. We can ask what happened to this gloriously mad religion of revolution, this topsy-turvy ass-instead-of-stallion point of view, when it became respectable and a part of the Establishment. A study of this particular period of Church History helps us towards answering the question which burns into the consciousness in the lands of the young Churches, but which applies equally in Europe and America, that is, how much of this so-called Christianity is essential and how much is mere Europeanism? The real triumph of a world of thought often comes after that world itself has perished. The epoch of Vasco da Gama is at an end, but westernism is only now effectively permeating the Chinese, the Indian, the African countryside. The Church has to live in a post-Theodosian world, but the ways of thought developed in the late fourth century have become almost an inextricable part of her. In giving Christianity to new peoples how easily missionaries since Theodosius' day have found themselves asking their converts to accept the view that one group of Christians (their own of course) is the only true Church, that others are pretty well criminal. We now all accept the view that Church affairs ultimately depend on material prosperity and a sound organizational and legal basis, but it was in the fourth century that such considerations became important. Too easily in our relationships with other religions our politeness is a matter of biding our time till we can get at their throats; the old Roman paganism was the first to succumb to this approach and to take a victim's revenge.

Constantine was the erratic genius who took the great decision to link

Church and State. His sons made such dire use of his ideas that Julian the Apostate could try to revive the old Graeco-Roman paganism. Julian's successors had to go slow. It was left to a smaller man than Constantine to take up the basic concepts and work them out in detail. Theodosius was an average man with some gifts as a soldier. Suddenly he was elevated to the pinnacle of power. We find him capable of ruthless, consistent and resolute action; yet he often appears inclined to postpone issues, to find irresolute compromises. Sometimes he can be accused of tergiversation. He makes an interesting psychological study, but remains an enigma. Around him are men and women ruthlessly seeking their own ends. Tremendous forces—economic, political, religious—seem to impel him forward to a given line of policy. Because of his very ordinariness, we are better able to appreciate this man's dilemma, which is the dilemma of us all. More often than not he has to choose—not between simple good and obvious evil—but between two evils, or between a good which leads to evil and an evil which leads to good. In nearly every case what he eventually chooses is seen to bring results both good and ill.

It was this average man in these difficult circumstances who had to make decisions which have permanently affected the Church. It was agreed that truth was unitary in a more than mathematical sense, though Christian thinking on the Trinity might have suggested that unity can be organically multiform. It was necessary to decide which was the one and only possible form of true religion and the Theodosian settlement remains the basis of orthodoxy to this day. Theodosius decided to use government coercion to harry deviationists and he was the first to do so successfully and consistently for so long. His example has not lacked imitators through the centuries. It was Theodosius who decided to inflict the death-blow to his religion's chief rival, but at the same time Graeco-Roman paganism handed over to her conqueror for preservation a great deal of the best and worst in her inheritance. Western man remains very much of a pagan. At a time when Christianity is being accused by some of being too much identified with a particular civilization and by others of not being sufficiently indigenous, we cannot disregard what Theodosius' policy can reveal concerning basic principles.

At the end of the fourth century Christianity became the religion of the majority. There was a mass movement into the Church. At the same time there was the flowering of the patristic literature. Few ages can boast greater names than those of Augustine, Ambrose, Nazianzen and Chrysostom. Yet it was at this time that one begins to catch a whiff of the self-opinionated arrogance which people inside and outside the Church sometimes mistake for an ingredient of catholicism. It was now that Christianity was made the religion of Christ-the-Giver-of-Victory (on the battlefield). When God gave the victory to others, Egypt, Roman Africa, Syria and later the western Mongols were lost to Christianity. But in the meantime, thousands had rushed in to benefit from this religion which was alleged to give success in battle, in harvest and even against epidemics. Was it the victory of Julian's Galilean?

It is the purpose of these pages to study the religious policy of Theodosius the Great in the hope that a little light will be shed on some of these perennially pressing problems. Naturally no cut-and-dried answers can be given and more questions will be raised than answered. Turgidity of style will, we hope, be forgiven one whose mother tongue was *babu* English and disjointedness and gaps and perhaps some inaccuracies to one who is of no fixed abode. Many references were jotted down on scraps of paper years ago, and it had been impossible to check them all. It is now eleven years since the writer began on and off to amuse his leisure moments with these studies. Many people have encouraged him when their advice should have been Mr Punch's to those about to marry. It was Dr G. W. H. Lampe, the present Ely Professor at Cambridge, who first suggested the topic and who has given much help. Dr Henry Chadwick, the present Regius Professor of Divinity at Oxford, read the work in manuscript and made many most valuable suggestions. The work has also had the benefit of criticism and suggestions by Dr S. L. Greenslade, the Regius Professor of Ecclesiastical History at Oxford. The writer has also received help from Professors N. H. Baynes, A. H. M. Jones, F. L. Cross, Claude Jenkins, E. A. Thompson; Dr J. N. D. Kelly, Dr M. A. C. Warren and Dr Mary Hartley; Miss Molly Whittaker, Messrs C. E. Stevens, Ian Barton, H. M. Collard, Hereward King, David Edwards, Thomas Hodgkin, Father Gervase Matthew, O.P., Brother George Every, S.S.M., and many other scholars. It is a pleasure to thank the publishers, and especially Mr Michael King, for their generous patience, and also those who have laboured with the typing and technical aid by way of maps and photostats: Miss D. M. Collard, Fraulein Elspeth Lerch, Mr Ebenezer Mantey Amoah of Larteh-Akwapim, Mrs G. A. Snodgrass, and Mr Cartwright and Mr Welsh of Nottingham University. The Staffs of the Coin Rooms at the British Museum and the Ashmolean have helped generously. Having been nearly always away from the great and ancient Libraries I have drawn heavily on the patience of the Staffs of the Denman Library at Retford, the Library of the Society of the Sacred Mission at Kelham, the Cathedral Library at Lincoln, the University

Libraries at Nottingham, Achimota and Legon in Ghana, as well as the admirable service of the National Central Library. Lastly I must thank those kindly patrons of learning, the Universities of Oxford, Nottingham and Ghana, as well as my wife and children and the parish and people of Shelford, Notts., for providing the background in which scholarship flourishes.

Legon, Ghana,   N. Q. KING
Die Philippi Quaque, 1960

ABBREVIATIONS

CIL	*Corpus Inscriptionum Latinarum.*
CSEL	*Corpus Scriptorum Ecclesiasticorum Latinorum.*
Chron.Min.	*Chronica Minora*, ed. T. Mommsen, 2 vols, Berlin, 1892 and 1894.
DACL	*Dictionnaire d'archéologie chrétienne et de liturgie.*
FHG	*Fragmenta Historicum Graecorum.*
HTR	*Harvard Theological Review.*
JTS	*Journal of Theological Studies.*
Mansi	J. D. Mansi, *Sacrorum conciliorum nova et amplissima collectio* III, Florence, 1759.
Orosius	Orosius, *Historiarum adversus paganos libri VIII*, ed. C. Zangemeister, Vienna, 1882.
Pacatus	Pacatus, *Panegyricus* in *XII Panegyrici Latini*, ed. G. Baehrens, Leipzig, 1874.
Paulinus	Paulinus, *Vita Ambrosii.*
PW	*Realencyclopädie der klassischen Altertumswissenschaft*, ed. W. Pauly, G. Wissowa and W. Kroll, Stuttgart, 1893 ff.
Pearce	J. W. E. Pearce, *Valentinian I to Theodosius I (Roman Imperial Coinage* IX), London, 1951.
Philostorgius	Fragments of Philostorgius' *Historia Ecclesiastica*, ed. J. Bidez, in *Griech. Chr. Schrift.* XXI, Leipzig, 1913.
RAC	*Reallexikon für Antike und Christentum*, ed. T. Klauser, Stuttgart, 1950 ff.
Rauschen	G. Rauschen, *Jahrbücher der christlichen Kirche unter dem Kaiser Theodosius dem Grossen*, Freiburg, 1897.
Rufinus	*Historia Ecclesiastica* in *Griech. Chr. Schrift.* IX 2 (Eusebius II 2), Leipzig 1908.
Socrates	Socrates, *Historia Ecclesiastica.*
Sozomen	Sozomen, *Historia Ecclesiastica.*
Theodoret	Theodoret, *Historia Ecclesiastica.*
ZNTW	*Zeitschrift für die neutestamentliche Wissenschaft.*
Zosimus	Zosimus, *Historia Nova*, ed. L. Mendelssohn, Leipzig, 1887.
XVI : 1 : 1 (or any triple numeration standing by itself)	*Codex Theodosianus*, liber XVI, *titulus* 1, *lex* 1; in *Theodosiani libri XVI*, ed. T. Mommsen and P. M. Meyer, 3 vols in 2, Berlin, 1905 ff.

Unless otherwise specified, the edition of the Fathers used is that of J. P. Migne (*PL* for the Latin, *PG* for the Greek).

I

Introduction

THE CALL, THE MAN AND HIS INHERITANCE

IN THE year 378 the Goths destroyed the flower of the Roman army in the plains outside Hadrianople. The Arian Emperor Valens took shelter in a hut and lost his life when it was set alight by the enemy.[1] In this dire emergency the young Gratian, who was now senior Augustus, summoned from his home in Spain a certain Theodosius whom he elevated to the purple in the January of 379.[2]

This Theodosius had been born some 32 years before at Cauca, which is north of Toledo. He was a scion of no mean house, and his family owned extensive lands. His parents were probably Christian, for his father while awaiting execution asked for baptism. Orosius notes that he was baptized a Nicene. Socrates and Sozomen say that Theodosius was brought up a follower of the homoousian faith.[3] No doubt Theodosius had been brought up as a western Christian of the day. This probably means that the theology of his teachers was implicitly based on the teaching of the western fathers since Tertullian, that the Son was 'of one substance' with the Father.

The *Epitome de Caesaribus* informs us that Theodosius was so called as a result of a dream, for he was God-given. This story probably applies to Theodosius' father who was of the same name. From it we may suppose that the family was pious, but in days when pagans were tending towards monotheism, the name is not necessarily Christian. It appears that Theodosius was only moderately well educated in a literary way, but he had a strong liking for the history of the ancients.[4] No doubt his main education

[1] Orosius VII 33; Rufinus XII 13.
[2] The detailed chronology of this reign is full of difficulties which have been sufficiently discussed in Rauschen and O. Seeck's *Regesten der Kaiser und Päpste*. Our chronology follows theirs; only when they differ on matters vital to the argument or are doubtful is the chronology discussed in detail.
[3] Orosius VII 33; Socrates V 6; Sozomen VII 4.
[4] *Epitome de Caesaribus* XLVIII (in Pichlmayr's ed. of Aurelius Victor, Leipzig, 1911).

B

was the university of military service. The son fought under the father in Britain and against the Alemanni. Then he achieved independent command and obtained a quite notable victory over the barbarians.[1]

The father was sent to Africa to put down the revolt of Firmus. Here he waged campaigns marked by brilliant generalship, cruelty, and some success. He was suddenly put to death on imperial orders.[2] The young Theodosius laid down his office and returned to his estates in Spain. Here he married his first wife Flaccilla, and here his eldest son, Arcadius, was born.[3] Like Cincinnatus he was called to the rescue, as it were from the plough, in his fatherland's hour of need. The effect on his mind of the sudden reversal of his fortunes must have been great.[4] A man becoming Emperor in such circumstances would believe that he was called of God, and owed this God allegiance and faithful obedience.[5]

His predecessors had set before Theodosius a number of precedents he could follow in his religious policy, and a summary, inevitably grotesque, must be attempted. On becoming a follower of Christ Constantine took it for granted that he should play a full part in the life of the Church. He showered favours upon her, tried to find out what was best for her and used the normal imperial methods to carry forward his policy. He made it fairly clear to non-Christians that he thought they were wrong, but the pagans were still too powerful for him to do much against them. His son Constans, who ruled in the west, followed the same kind of policy but when the Donatists in Africa became troublesome and the revolutionary character of their movement became apparent, he used bribes, threats, then naked force. Constantius, the son who ruled in the east, and afterwards become sole Emperor, was in a great hurry. He inclined to Arian views and harried his ecclesiastical opponents with deportations, military attacks in church and imprisonment. He launched a violent attack on paganism. His nephew, Julian, restored the sacrifices and tried to revive paganism. Officially he returned to a policy of parity between the two religions but he attacked Christianity by such methods

---

[1] Pacatus VIII, Zosimus IV 35, Socrates V 2.

[2] Probably in 376. Ammianus Marcellinus, *Rerum gestarum* xxix.5.1–55; Orosius VII 33.

[3] Pacatus IX, Theodoret V 5, Socrates VI 23; cf. Claudian, *Laus Seren.*, lines 111–13. Ambrose (*De obitu Theodosii* 53) indicates that he nearly lost his life at the hands of those who killed his father.

[4] Theodoret (V 5) says he served a short time in a lower capacity before being made Augustus. Cf. Themistius *Or.* XIV (p. 182 in Dindorf ed.); *Epitome de Caesaribus* XLVII and Pacatus X. In any case, the promotion was rapid.

[5] Cf. Pacatus III and the coin types: 'Emperor raising kneeling turreted woman' with the legend REPARATIO-REIPUB, and 'Emperor crowned by a heavenly hand' (Pearce, pp. 300 and 257). See also Themistius, *Or.* XIV (p. 182), XVIII (p. 217).

as trying to keep her out of higher education and by granting privileges to paganism. He died before his policy could mature. The army, significantly enough, chose a Christian to follow Julian. This Jovian instituted a regime of genuine toleration and non-interference which was continued after his death by Valentinian I.[1] Writers both Christian and pagan agree with Ammian's conclusion that he stood in a middle position with regard to differences of religion. He disquieted no one, nor commanded any to worship this or that, nor did he use minatory interdicts to incline the necks of his subjects to that which he himself believed, but he left these parts of life undisturbed as he found them.[2] Early in his reign Valentinian consigned the East to his brother Valens. The brothers feared any religious practices which might be to their political disadvantage. Thus for instance though they did not consider haruspicy or any other religious practice allowed by the ancestors to be criminal, and they had allowed complete freedom to every individual to worship according to his personal convictions, they had to prohibit the use of haruspicy for harmful purposes.[3] For the same reasons they forbade bloody sacrifice, though the rest of pagan worship could continue.[4] Valens did not maintain the principle of non-interference when it came to dealing with Christians. He returned to a policy rather like that of Constantius, inclining towards a modified Arianism, and harrying his opponents with threats and exile.

In terms of the relationship between Church and State the policies so far mentioned and the reactions to them may be classified between two extremes.[5] There was the 'totalitarian' view set forth by Eusebius, aptly caricatured by Athanasius' picture of Constantius shouting 'Let my will be the canon'. The Emperor had brought with him into Christianity a

[1] See the writer's '*Compelle intrare* and the plea of the pagans', to be published in *The Modern Churchman*, in which the appeals for freedom of religion made by Themistius in *Oratio* V (delivered before Jovian), by Libanius in *Oratio* XXX and Symmachus in *Relatio* III are examined.

[2] Ammian xxx.9.5: '*Postremo hoc moderamine principatus inclaruit, quod inter religionum diversitates medius stetit, nec quemquam inquietavit, neque ut hoc coleretur imperavit aut illud: nec interdictis minacibus subiectorum cervicem ad id, quod ipse coluit, inclinabat, sed intemeratas reliquit has partes ut repperit.*' Cf. Zosimus IV 3, Socrates IV 1, Sozomen VI 6. Ammian was writing in Theodosius' day and there can be little doubt whose threatenings he has in mind.

[3] IX : 16 : 9—'*Haruspicinam ego nullum cum maleficiorum causis habere consortium iudico neque ipsam aut aliquam praeterea concessam a maioribus religionem genus esse arbitror criminis. Testes sunt leges a me in exordio imperii mei datae, quibus unicuique, quod animo inbibisset, colendi libera facultas tributa est. Nec haruspicinam reprehendimus, sed nocenter exerceri vetamus.*'

[4] Libanius, *Or.* XXX 7. Cf. IX : 16 : 7 and 8, and Zosimus IV 3.

[5] Convenient summaries in English will be found in S. L. Greenslade, *Church and State from Constantine to Theodosius*, London, 1954, and in T. M. Parker, *Christianity and the State in the light of History*, London, 1955.

sacral position which made him little less than divine.[1] On the Christian side, many parts of the ante-Nicene writings and of the New Testament assured men of the divine origin of the State. The Christian Emperor could soon be assimilated to the godly prince of the Old Testament.

At the other pole is Valentinian's steadfast refusal to meddle. Church and State existed side by side. This dual approach had the support of some pagan thinkers and of some of the sayings of men like Athanasius and Donatus, when they found the imperial rod on their own backs. It was a possible interpretation of the dominical 'Render unto Caesar'. Of course Valentinian's view was not that of the modern liberal; it was probably that of many a sergeant-major—superstitious fear of the supernatural, a desire for good order and discipline coupled with the belief that 'all roads is the same'. The trouble with such an approach is that it cannot be maintained in the face of a totalitarian government unless the head of that government himself enforces it. Again, Christianity cannot be hedged in: if you ask it just to keep to the 'spiritual' you emasculate it; its concern is the whole of life. The Church too can tend towards its own type of totalitarianism, as we shall discover when we come to discuss the views of St Ambrose and look forward into the history of the western Church in the Middle Ages.

The reader must decide for himself which side Theodosius was on, and not prejudge the issue because the man has the name of an autocrat who had to be humbled by the Church. As we piece together his policy we shall find him veering now to one side then to the other, but when it comes to making a conclusion we may discover that his approach was not an approximation to either nor a compromise dictated by expediency, but a fruitful and distinct approach.

Before coming to examine the policy of Theodosius something must be said of the policy of Gratian, who though a younger and in many ways a less powerful man, had preceded Theodosius on the throne by four years, had called him to it and then ruled the west for four years after his accession. In his dealings with the pagans, Gratian is said to have refused the title Pontifex Maximus, to have disendowed the sacred colleges, and to have removed the altar (not the statue) of Victory from the Senate House. The sources do not imply that the three actions took place together, so we may deal with each separately. Our sole source for the rejection of the title Pontifex Maximus is Zosimus, a man who as an

[1] In *There's such divinity doth hedge a King*, (Nelson, Edinburgh, for the University of Ghana, 1960), the writer has attempted to analyse some of the elements, Persian, Egyptian, Jewish, Hellenistic, Roman and Christian, which contributed to the ruler-cult and the religion of Kingship in the late fourth century.

historian is a pagan counterpart of Theodoret. They are veritable thorns in the flesh when one is trying to discover historical truth. He states that when each Emperor took over the rule of all things, the priestly stole was offered to him by the Pontiffs, and straightway he was written up as Pontifex Maximus. All the other Emperors had received the honour and had used the title, even when the Empire came to Constantine and he chose the faith of the Christians, turning aside from the right way in things to do with the divine. Even after this man, the others in succession did the same, including both Valentinian and Valens. So when the Pontiffs, according to their wont, brought the stole to Gratian, he rejected their request, considering that a Christian should not adopt such garb. Zosimus says that the head of the Pontiffs remarked as the stole was returned to them, that if he did not wish to be Pontifex, there would soon be created a Pontifex, Maximus.[1]

While it is not possible to date this incident accurately because of the lack of chronological data,[2] the chances are that Theodosius' accession took place before Gratian rejected the title.[3] Although it is an argument from silence, we are on safe ground if we say Theodosius never bore the title. In his case it might well have been a failure to assume, rather than a determination to reject. This failure may not have been caused by religious considerations. The title, after all, had Republican associations, and he seems to have dropped other Republican titles.

We turn now to consider Gratian's disendowment of the priestly colleges. A law promulgated by Honorius in 415 refers to a constitution of the late Gratian which ordered that all places set aside by the error of the ancients for sacred rites, should be made over to the Emperor's possession. The Emperor refers to the time when it was forbidden to spend public money on superstition.[4] This law justifies us in thinking that Gratian ordered that the public was no longer to support pagan religious expenditure, and that certain pagan holy places were to be taken over by the Imperial exchequer. The pagan Symmachus and St Ambrose

---

[1] Zosimus IV 37. A comma has been inserted in the last sentence to bring out the pun. The reference to Maximus indicates that Zosimus thought the incident took place fairly close to Maximus' mutiny.

[2] Scholars attempt it just the same, see for instance: A. Alföldi, *A Festival of Isis*, Budapest, 1937, pp. 36 f.; J. R. Palanque in *Byzantion* VIII, 1939, pp. 41 ff.; McGuire, *Catholic Historical Review* XXII, 1936, pp. 304 ff.; and W. Ensslin, *Die Religionspolitik des Kaisers Theodosius*, Munich, 1953, pp. 9 f.

[3] In 379 we find Ausonius playing on the word 'Pontifex' in his *Gratiarum actio* (*PL* 19, col. 942 f.). He could not have done so had Gratian so pointedly already rejected the title. Theodosius was elevated at the very beginning of the year.

[4] XVI : 10 : 20—'. . . *Omnia etiam loca, quae sacris error veterum deputavit, secundum divi Gratiani constituta nostrae rei iubemus sociari ita ut ex eo tempore, quo inhibitus est publicus sumptus superstitioni deterrimae exhiberi, fructus ab incubatoribus exigantur . . .*'

give us further information. Symmachus, speaking some years after Gratian's death, says that the Vestal Virgins have lost certain exemptions. Priests have suffered losses, the profits of which have gone to the Treasury and to the maintenance of the *cursus publicus*. Bequests to sacred bodies have been taken over, and the public does not any longer maintain them. St Ambrose says that if Valentinian II does what the pagans ask he will be restoring a system by which money is given for pagan sacrifices, a system which was abolished by Gratian. This abolition has enriched the Emperor. The Vestals have lost privileges but these have not been transferred to the Christian virgins. Their priests are no longer supported by the public and they have lost land.[1] St Ambrose points out that the pagans still had more privileges than the Christians. These measures equalized, to some extent, the ministers of the two religions. They seem to have been prompted by a desire to fill the Treasury, as much as by any anti-pagan motive. The old religious practices were free to continue as before, but at private expense.[2]

The same letters of Ambrose suggest that the altar of Victory which was removed from the Senate House by Gratian probably in 382, was taken away to allow fair and equal treatment for the Christian members of the Senate.[3] Gratian could hardly have intended to put a stop to the idea of the Roman dependence on Victory. The statue was left intact, and without the altar it could be accepted by the Christians as an angel or by the pagans as a goddess. With the altar in place it was unequivocally a goddess, and even if they did not sprinkle incense they were bound to see and smell the accursed thing.

It is clear that Gratian did nothing spectacular against paganism before 379 when St Ambrose established an ascendancy over his mind. Even when he took such steps, his policy still remained within the limits of the official parity which was supposed to exist between the two religions.

We must turn now to consider Gratian's dealings with the Christians. During the first years of his sovereign rule in the west (375 to 378), he seems to have continued his father's policy of non-intervention in church affairs as long as peace was preserved. In 376 he did indeed order the Proconsul of Africa to confiscate the places where the heretics had altars, but this probably refers to the Donatists, who were notorious troublers of

---

[1] Symmachus, *Relatio* III 8, 11–15. Ambrose, *Ep.* XVII 3–9, 16; *Ep.* XVIII 10 f., 16, 31. Cf. *De obitu Valentiniani* 19 f.

[2] *CIL* VI.2158 shows that the College of Pontiffs carried out certain repairs at their own expense; cf. VI.754.

[3] For instance, *Ep.* XVII 9 f. Concerning the dating to 382, in *Ep.* XVII 10, which was written in 384, St Ambrose refers to an appeal to Gratian two years before, soon after the removal of the altar.

the peace.[1] In 378 Gratian moved out of Gaul to assist his uncle against the Goths. He seems now to have been confronted with Arianism for the first time. He wrote to St Ambrose for help and advice. The Emperor and the bishop met at Sirmium and so began a friendship which lasted till the former's death. The policy of toleration was continued for the moment. When Valens died in battle, Gratian issued an edict which allowed religious exiles to return home and made every Christian worship free, with the exception of the Eunomian, Photinian and Manichaean.[2] Also during the period between Valens' death and the elevation of Theodosius, Gratian issued the rescript *ordinariorum sententias*.[3] A synod at Rome had accepted the Tome of Damasus which included the Nicene Creed. The Council anathematized the Sabellians, Arians, Eunomians, Macedonians and Photinians, together with those who teach a doctrine of two Sons (certain Antiochenes?) those who deny that the Word took a rational and intelligent soul (the Apollinarians?) and those who believe in the expansion and contraction of the godhead (the Marcellians?). They sent two suggestions to the Emperor. If a bishop had been condemned by the Pope or by the Roman Synod, the Emperor should exile him; a bishop summoned to Rome should be compelled to come. Secondly, the Bishop of Rome should not come under the jurisdiction of any normal court save that of the Emperor. In replying, Gratian was most reluctant to harness Church and State together. He granted the first requests about the authority of the Roman see over other bishops in his domains, but answered the second about the Pope's appeal to his court vaguely.

It would seem then that during the fateful months at the end of 378 and in the first weeks of 379 when Gratian decided to send for Theodosius and to raise him to the purple, his policy was not strongly directed in the

---

[1] XVI : 5 : 4 to Hesperius the Praetorian Prefect. Piganiol (*L'Empire chrétien*, p. 207) rightly points out that he was Proconsul of Africa and suggests the connection with the Donatists.

[2] The edict itself is not extant, but XVI : 5 : 5 refers to it and details are given in Socrates V 2 and Sozomen VII 1. Rufinus (XII 13) says Valens allowed the return of the exiles, his evidence is contradicted by XVI : 5 : 5. He was probably misled by the slipping back of some exiles when Valens died. Theodoret (V 2) says Gratian sent a General Sapor at this time to put down Arianism and restore the Nicenes. The story is clearly Theodoret's own composition with its pedantic references to shepherds, flocks and wolves (bishops, congregations and Arians). He takes it that XVI : 5 : 6 of 381 is in force. Theodosius found the Arians very much at large. The mission of Sapor could not have taken place till 381 and without any hint of support from other sources, it seems best to consider it as a fabrication based on bazaar gossip. Gratian's policy is fully treated in F. Homes Dudden, *The life and times of St Ambrose*, and J. R. Palanque, *S. Ambroise et l'empire romain*.

[3] *Collectio Avellana* XIII; *CSEL* XXXV, pp. 54 ff. See also Hefele-Leclerq, *Histoire des conciles* I 2, p. 984; C. H. Turner, *Ecclesiae occidentalis monumenta iuris antiquissima* I, pp. 281 ff., T. Jalland, *The Church and the Papacy*, pp. 244 ff.

Nicene direction. Also he was obviously not desirous of meddling in the Church's affairs. We do not know what instructions he gave Theodosius. In any case it was up to the latter to do the task entrusted to him and he would go about it as he thought fit.

If Theodosius in his first years took a strong line in church affairs, it cannot be said he inherited this from Gratian for not till the summer of 379 did the latter depart from the policy of *laissez faire*. While on a visit to Milan at that time he withdrew his edict of toleration and ordered all heresies to be silent. He especially attacked those who under the name of bishops, priests and deacons spread opinions which diminished the notion of the godhead (presumably the Arian ministry) and those who re-baptized (presumably the Donatists).[1] Gratian thus began a policy of steady support for St Ambrose which was to endure till his death.

On the face of it, it looks as if Gratian's influence on Theodosius could not have been great. It must also be borne in mind that relations between the two Emperors soon deteriorated till they were in a state little short of war.[2] Yet it is possible that Gratian had already made up his mind about religion in 378 and that part of Theodosius' qualification as a suitable colleague was the likelihood that in matters religious they would see eye to eye. Even after political relationships had grown hostile, in religion they could quite well be in accord. The evidence for this will be examined as it appears.

We may now consider the immediate situation Theodosius faced in the eastern church. The situation was most confused, much like a sea fight in a fog.[3] Two Nicene groups had now emerged. The 'old Nicenes' could look back to the teachings of Eustathius of Antioch with its emphasis on the oneness of the Trinity, as their own. They were in communion with Rome and Alexandria and had never attempted compromise. The 'young Nicenes' were Cappadocian in their theology but some of them had a doubtful history of relationships with men whose orthodoxy had been suspect. The leader of this group was Meletius who had been translated to Antioch in 360. Both Constantius and Valens had exiled him for not being Arian enough, yet Athanasius and the west had consistently rejected him despite the support given him by Basil the Great and most of the oriental bishops. Now Meletius was to become one of the main

---

[1] XVI : 5 : 5.

[2] See Seeck, *Geschichte* V, pp. 166 ff. After all, Gratian's family had executed Theodosius' father and rusticated the son. More important was the reassertion of eastern independence of the west (the numismatic evidence is conclusive: Pearce, pp. xix f.).

[3] Professor H. Chadwick drew the writer's attention to the aptness of Basil, *De Spiritu Sancto* XXX 76 f. as a description of the situation.

architects of the settlement associated with the Second Oecumenical Council. Meletius started on an immediate reorganization of his own church area.[1]

In the autumn of 379, Meletius called a council of 153 bishops at Antioch.[2] It would seem that Meletius of Antioch, Eusebius of Samosata, Pelagius of Laodicea, Zeno of Tyre, Eulogius of Edessa, Bematius 'de Mallo' and Diodore of Tarsus, together with 146 oriental bishops, subscribed. The Council agreed to the teaching set forth in four letters sent at various times by the bishops of the west. Herein they accepted the oneness of the deity and substance of the Trinity, and the full deity of the Holy Spirit, while they rejected teachings which are associated with the Apollinarians, Pneumatomachoi and the Marcellians.[3] The Council also probably accepted a creed or doctrinal statement in credal form.[4] The probability would be increased if a creed were to hand which might fit the situation. Dr Telfer draws our attention to item XXIII of the Verona Codex, where a creed is given under the obviously erroneous title 'The Creed of Sardica'. He associates the creed with Antioch and concludes: 'These considerations confirm us in seeking the origin of the creed of item XXIII in Syria and before 379. And if this is right, the influence of Meletius, rather than that of Cyril of Jerusalem, is the real clue to the Constantinopolitanum.'[5]

To conclude with regard to the Council of Antioch 379, it may be said to have been a continuation of Basil's attempts at reconciliation. The first

---

[1] Theodoret V 4. He or his friends installed some nine of their comrades in neighbouring sees who appeared at the council of 381 in his support.

[2] Gregory of Nyssa, *De vita S. Macrinae* (*PG* 46 col. 973d); E. Schwartz, 'Zur Geschichte des Athanasius', *Nachrichten v. d. kgl. Gesellschaft d. Wissen. zu Göttingen*, phil.-hist. Kl., 1904, pp. 357 ff.; *ZNTW* XXXIV, 1935, p. 198, and XXXV, 1936, pp. 1 ff. We know something of the decisions of this council thanks to the collection of Theodosius the Deacon in Codex Veronensis LX (58); see W. Telfer, *HTR* XXXVI, 1943, pp. 169 ff.; C. H. Turner, *Ecclesiae occidentalis monumenta* I, pp. 625 ff.; the Ballerini (*PL* 56 col. 143 ff.); Merenda (*PL* 13 col. 347 ff.); C. H. Turner in *JTS* XXX, 1929, pp. 113 ff.

[3] On these letters see also Sozomen VI 23 and Theodoret II 17; E. Schwartz, *Nachrichten v. d. Kgl.*, 1904, pp. 364 ff.; and Bardy in *Revue Bénédictine*, 1933, pp. 199 ff. The Apollinarians denied the existence of the highest human element in the incarnate Lord. The Pneumatomachoi were those who refused full deity to the Holy Spirit. Marcellus of Ancyra (*ob.* 374), a staunch supporter of the Nicenes, had taught that the Godhead was a monad which expanded into a triad for the purpose of creation and salvation but would contract again at the End-time.

[4] One cannot be certain of this because of the ambiguity of the words *fides* and τόμος. The redactor of the letters and bishop list in the Verona Codex says they consented to 'the *fides* set out above', while the Fathers at Constantinople in 382 refer to a τόμος of Antioch in which they confessed their faith (Theodoret V 9). The Patmian Canon XVIII also refers to a τόμος set forth at Antioch which laid down the homoousion of the Trinity. (On these Canons see Appendix B and C. H. Turner, *JTS* XV, 1914, pp. 161 ff.)

[5] *HTR* XXXVI, 1943, pp. 169 ff.

and most pressing task was to bring about reconciliation with the west. Clearly Meletius had looked out everything he could find by Damasus and had accepted it in the hope that the Pope would accept him. But it was not only a matter of doctrine, order too was involved. The west could not agree that Meletius had a better claim than Paulinus to be the legitimate Bishop of Antioch. On the other hand the Council of Antioch made no compromise in the matter of persons—there was no question but that Meletius was Bishop of Antioch, and not Paulinus.

Meletius had other rivals at Antioch beside Paulinus. The Apollinarian Vitalis gave him little trouble, for he was junior in years of episcopate, clearly schismatically consecrated, and his views had been expressly condemned more than once.[1] The Arian Dorotheus who had succeeded Euzoius in 376 was not in a very strong position once he lost official support. There is no need to suppose that his party at Antioch was in any way repressed by official action at this time; Meletius clearly had the people behind him and the Arians were left high and dry.

The position of Tyre is rather difficult to grasp. Rufinus says that Meletius' faction at Tyre ousted Diodore, a Nicene of the old school like Paulinus of Antioch, and inserted another man.[2] This was presumably the Zeno of Tyre who attended Constantinople 381. The difficulty is that a Zeno signed for Tyre in the Nicene list of 325, and it is not beyond the bounds of human longevity that the same man attended both the first and second oecumenical Councils. Possibly the Zeno of 381 was the son of the Zeno of 325, or the original Zeno was still alive and had joined the Meletian group.

At Jerusalem Cyril was in possession of the episcopate.[3] At Caesarea, beside Gelasius, there was an Arian bishop named Euzoius who was not driven out till later in the reign.[4] At Alexandria, Peter, the successor of Athanasius, had been able to slip back after Valens left Antioch. The mob arose and drove out his opponent, the Arian Lucius, who retired to the friendly background of Constantinople.[5]

Turning to the west coast of Asia Minor, we find that the 'Macedonians' had entered into negotiation with the westerners and had been received back into communion. When Gratian's edict of toleration was

[1] Schwartz, ZNTW XXXIV, 1935, p. 197.
[2] XI 21.
[3] Socrates V 3; Jerome, De viris illustribus CXII.
[4] Jerome, Viris illustr. CXIII. Euzoius was probably ejected as a result of XVI : 5 : 6 of 381.
[5] Socrates IV 37; Sozomen VI 38. Jerome (Viris illustr. CXVIII) says Theodosius drove Lucius from Alexandria. The reputation of the Christian plebs at Alexandria, and the fear of lynching, are probably enough to explain the bishop's hasty departure.

promulgated, they met at Antioch in Caria and returned to the homoe-ousian faith.[1] They seem to have decided to remain separate from the homoousian party, but there was good hope of reconciling them. At Constantinople, since the days of Constantius II, the Church had been in the hands of the Arians. They had used their advantage well, and by the time Theodosius came to the throne, the Arian bishop Demo-philus had genuine popular support. But Demophilus' fall was being prepared. A deputation on behalf of the poor little remnant of a Nicene flock waited on St Gregory of Nazianzus, and invited him to be their bishop. After a certain hesitation, he accepted and began that work at the Anastasia which was to do so much to build up a Nicene congrega-tion.[2]

During this time there came from Alexandria a former cynic philo-sopher, by name Maximus, who ingratiated himself with the gullible Gregory. Then, with the help of some bishops from Egypt, he had him-self clandestinely consecrated Bishop of Constantinople. The people rose against him and drove him out. He went to Theodosius, but was re-buffed.[3] St Gregory himself is our main source in this account, and he clearly wants to make out that Maximus was nothing but a charlatan and an adventurer. Yet this strange person had behind him the support of the Bishop of Alexandria. No group of Egyptian bishops would have come to the consecration without the command of the Pope of Alexandria. The whole plot is of a piece with the later methods of the Bishops of Alexandria, except that Peter did not appear in person, while Theo-philus, Cyril and Dioscorus did their own dirty work. Maximus was bishop long enough to ordain clerics, and a sufficiently episcopal figure to cause Ambrose to believe in him. The judicious Damasus was not, however, taken in.[4]

Such then was the inheritance of Theodosius when he took over the imperial part in religious affairs in the eastern regions of the Roman Empire. It is now possible to examine his own religious policy.

[1] Sozomen VII 2; Socrates V 4. The 'Macedonians' were defective in their doctrine of the Holy Spirit. Their connection with Macedonius the Bishop of Constantinople is not proven. They may have obtained their name from their exegesis of Acts 16.6–10.

[2] Gregory Nazianzen, *De se ipso et de episcopis*, lines 81 ff. (*PG* 37 col. 1172); *De vita sua*, lines 607 ff. (1071 ff.); Socrates V 6. *De vita*, lines 652–78 tells of an attack on him when celebrating the Eucharist.

[3] *De vita*, lines 750 ff. Gregory's *Oratio* XXV is in praise of Maximus. See also Jerome, *Viris illustr.* CXVII.

[4] Sozomen VII 9; Constantinople 381 Canon IV; Ambrose, *Ep.* XIII; Damasus, *Epp.* V and VII. Theodoret (V 8) says one of Maximus' consecrators was Timothy. A man of that name succeeded Peter as Bishop of Alexandria.

2

The Catholic and Oecumenical Settlement

THE FIRST YEARS OF IMPERIAL POWER

THEODOSIUS OPENED his campaign against all the heresies with the magnificent trumpet blast of the edict *Cunctos populos*.[1] The Emperor commanded all the peoples under his rule to follow that form of religion which had been handed by the Apostle Peter to the Romans. It was followed by the Pontifex Damasus and Peter, Bishop of Alexandria. According to the apostolic discipline and evangelical teaching, we should believe that the Father, the Son and the Holy Spirit are one godhead in equal majesty and in pious Trinity. Those who accepted this law should take to themselves the name of Catholic Christians, the rest were declared to be mad and savage men. They were to bear the infamy of being heretics, and their conventicles were not to have the name of churches. They would be stricken first by the divine vengeance, and then by the Emperor's action against them which he would take in accordance with the decision of heaven.

In what is probably part of the same edict the Emperor stated 'those who confuse the divine law by ignorance, or violate and offend it by neglect, commit sacrilege'.[2]

[1] XVI : 1 : 2 to the people of Constantinople from Thessalonica in February 380: '*Cunctos populos, quos clementiae nostrae regit temperamentum, in tali volumus religione versari, quam divinum Petrum apostolum tradidisse Romanis religio usque ad nunc ab ipso insinuata declarat quamque pontificem Damasum sequi claret et Petrum Alexandriae episcopum virum apostolicae sanctitatis, hoc est, ut secundum apostolicam disciplinam euangelicamque doctrinam patris et filii et spiritus sancti unam deitatem sub parili maiestate et sub pia trinitate credamus. Hanc legem sequentes Christianorum catholicorum nomen iubemus amplecti, reliquos vero dementes vesanosque iudicantes haeretici dogmatis infamiam sustinere nec conciliabula eorum ecclesiarum nomen accipere, divina primum vindicta post etiam motus nostri, quem ex caelesti arbitrio sumpserimus, ultione plectendos.*' Cf. Sozomen VII 4 and Philostorgius IX 19.

[2] XVI : 2 : 25 of the same date, place and superscription, but without address, was placed by the compilers of the Code under section 2 of Book XVI. They were permitted to do this under their terms of reference.

As with most trumpet blasts, nobody paid any attention once the noise ceased. Demophilus the Arian remained in possession of the churches. St Gregory Nazianzen, struggling for the Nicene cause, does not so much as mention it. The Emperor himself departed from its details. Rather than its effects, it is the thought of this law which is important. The rhythmic beauty and sonorous dignity of the wording warn us that we have before us the work of the imperial *scrinia*, but even so the law gives us some valuable clues to the thinking of Theosodius in what is, as it were, his election manifesto and speech from the throne.[1]

Theodosius clearly believes that he has received his power from heaven. There is one true form of religion which has come down from the Apostles and it is upheld by the Bishops of Rome and Alexandria, and by Scripture. Those who do not follow this law (that is, faith) have outlawed themselves, they have lost their rights as citizens of the Roman and of the Christian Empire. They will certainly be smitten by God, and by the Emperor, who is God's agent. For Theodosius, then, citizenship and orthodoxy, imperially dictated right belief and Catholicism are being aligned.[2]

Before leaving the edict one must observe that Theodosius seems to have come down on the side of the west in taking Rome and Alexandria as his touchstones of orthodoxy. Meletius and the easterners, had they ever seen the edict, might justly have felt alarmed, even if they made full allowance for the possibility that the position in the east was still so uncertain from the Emperor's point of view that he could not find any sufficiently unchallenged easterner to name. Had Theodosius maintained this position his task of bringing peace to the Church would have been made hopeless from the beginning. We shall see how he quietly dropped his brash western ways and conformed to the ways of thought of his own dominions.

In considering what might have been the background of the Emperor's thinking when this edict was drafted, it is worthwhile to note the staggering impact his sudden change of fortune in 378-9 must have had on his

---

[1] On the civil and military sides its counterpart is perhaps the Aes II type, GLORIA RO-MANORUM, 'Emperor standing on ship with right hand raised; Victory at the helm', issued at eastern mints in the early years of Theodosius (Pearce, pp. 225 f.).

[2] Professor H. Chadwick drew the writer's attention to C. C. J. Webb's remarks about Christianity's 'new intellectualism in the form of what came to be called orthodoxy' (*Christianity's Contribution to Ethics*, Calcutta, 1932, pp. 48 ff.). Webb notes the close connection between the high estimate of the value of orthodoxy and the practice of persecution, and concludes: 'it has always been difficult or nearly impossible to reconcile the temper which these principles demand with one which will strike most men as appropriate to the charity or love which the New Testament exalts as the chief and parent of all virtues.'

mind. Suddenly to become an Emperor surrounded by a religion of monarchy which made him almost superhuman would either give a man megalomania, or turn him to the task of finding out and implementing the will of the God whose power he wielded. There is something else which may have had a tremendous effect on the Emperor's mind during this time. Theodosius, like many other people who were going to serve their country by taking office, was not baptized as an infant. It was considered that office almost inevitably involved its holder in sin.[1] Sin did not seem to matter so much if the person concerned was not yet baptized, for baptism would wash all sin away. Constantine and Constantius were baptized on their death-beds. Poor Valentinian II was overtaken by death while unbaptized.[2] Probably it was Theodosius' intention to delay his baptism until his death-bed. But while at Thessalonica he fell ill, and as he expected to die he was baptized by Ascholius the bishop, who was a Nicene in belief. He recovered from the illness not many days afterwards and came to Constantinople.[3]

His baptism so early in his career as Emperor meant that during the greater part of his reign Theodosius was pledged to Christ in a way in which, for instance, Constantine and Constantius II had not been. Moreover, it placed Ascholius in a position to exercise great influence at a vital time over the mind of a person who, as we shall see, was liable to be controlled by those about him.[4] Ascholius was a bishop with strongly 'western' affinities. Pope Damasus looked to him to protect western interests at the Council of Constantinople in 381 and St Ambrose thought

---

[1] See the Canons of Elvira, and St Gregory Nazianzen, *Oratio* XL 19. Cf. St Augustine, *Confessions* I.xi.17. Modern Churches in Africa faced with the problems of chieftaincies which involve bloody offerings to ancestors and polygamy do not seem to have made official use of this device.

[2] F. J. Dölger, 'Die Taufe Konstantins', *Römische Quartalschrift* XIX, pp. 377 ff.; Athanasius, *De synodis* XXXI; Socrates II 47. Ambrose, *De obitu Valentiniani* 23, 25, 75.

[3] Socrates V 6. This normally reliable historian indicates that Theodosius was baptized towards the end of the year. In this case, *Cunctos populos* preceded the baptism. Sozomen (VII 4) considers the edict a result of the baptism. This is probably based on *a priori* reasoning, since it is what one would expect from a neophyte. W. Ensslin, *Die Religionspolitik des Kaisers Theodosius*, pp. 17 ff. and the review by Piganiol in *Byzantinische Zeitschrift* XLVI, 1955, pp. 390 ff., support Socrates' dating; cf. Schwartz, *ZNTW* XXXIV, 1935, p. 196 and Seeck, *Regesten*, pp. 253 f.; *Geschichte* V, p. 484. One cannot seriously base a dating on gaps in legislative activity indicated by the Code, working on the assumption that a gap indicates the Emperor's illness and the baptism followed the illness. The Code does not pretend to preserve every law promulgated. All one can do is to accept Socrates' dating relying on him as an historian and remembering it is the more difficult dating to invent.

[4] These 'influences' cover almost the entire reign—Ascholius, Meletius, Flaccilla, Cynegius, perhaps Justina through Galla, Ambrose, Rufinus. To admit that he was influenced by these people is not to imply that Theodosius was a weak man. Everybody's mind is swayed by those around him no matter how strong he is. Real strength lies in recognizing this and allowing for it.

highly of him.[1] Ascholius' point of view in religious matters would not differ much from that of the *coterie espagnole pieuse* which it has been suggested may have been around the Emperor.[2]

Within a few days of his arrival at Constantinople the Emperor sent for Demophilus, who was by succession the bishop of the city, but who was an Arian. The Bishop was told to accept the Nicene faith, and when he refused, he was turned out. With him went Lucius of Alexandria.[3] In Socrates' account the Emperor emphasizes the need for unity, peace and harmony, and he seems convinced that nothing will give this other than adherence to the Creed of Nicaea. Presumably, if Demophilus had dissembled and accepted Nicaea, he would have been left in possession, but not all Arians were made of the same stuff as the picture of the typical Arian given by Athanasius and Theodoret. Demophilus made no fuss; he felt he could not struggle with superior force, and so adjourned his meetings to places outside the walls.[4] Thus, as Socrates points out, the Arians, after holding the churches for forty years, were put out of the city. Some have seen in this a certain poetic justice—as Arianism was imposed by the Emperor, so it was removed. But Arianism was not just an intellectual creed of logicality for theologians, court bishops, and members of the upper classes; it had produced its saints and scholars, and in Ulfilas a man almost worthy of the name 'Apostle'. In Constantinople it had bitten deep, and Theodosius had still to reckon with its popular support.

Theodosius received St Gregory of Nazianzus graciously at their first interview. The Emperor considered that Gregory's works had earned him the church, and that it was the will of God that he should have it at the hand of the Emperor. Theodosius, by the use of force, then installed Gregory in the Church of the Apostles. Though Gregory would have us believe his mission to the city had been highly successful despite the mob violence of his opponents, there is no doubt that his followers were a minority. The soldiery had to protect their bishop from molestation as he went to the Church of the Apostles. St Gregory describes the scene—the

---

[1] Pope Damasus, *Ep.* V (*PL* 13 col. 365 ff.); Ambrose, *Ep.* XV.

[2] Piganiol, *L'Empire chrétien*, pp. 209, 217.

[3] Socrates V 7; Sozomen VII 5; Philostorgius IX 19; Ambrose, *Ep.* XII 1. Eunomius perhaps went out as well at this time, though Sozomen (VII 6) and Theodoret (V 16) show that Theodosius hesitated to strike at him.

[4] It is a great pity that Demophilus went quietly. Neither the Arians nor the pagans had any notion of the duty to resist the government when it acts wrongly; they produced no martyrs. Tatian, himself a pagan, was Praetorian Prefect of the East when some of the worst outrages against paganism were committed. In such circumstances, unarmed opposition, however hopeless of effect, is the only means of forcing the powers that be to reconsider what they are doing.

streets, the hippodromes and squares were full, there were tears and looks of sorrow as if it were the triumphal progress of an enemy. The Emperor marched to the church with his guard, and with them, an incongruous figure, scarcely breathing, shuffled St Gregory Nazianzen. He was a little cheered when the clouds lifted, for this perhaps indicated that heaven was more pleased than the crowd.[1] So St Gregory was installed in the chief church of the capital.

This is one of the few first-hand accounts that we have of Theodosius in action, implementing his policy towards the Christian Church at the point of the sword. One shares in St Gregory's mixed feelings of humiliation and bewilderment, together with his underlying knowledge that it was the will of God that the Nicene faith should triumph. It is difficult for us to understand the adoption of force by a Christian to produce religious conformity when such methods so flatly contradict the teaching of the New Testament, but the attempt must be made. The Emperors might well have thought that deviationists could not be allowed to upset the unity and good order of the Church. Besides, their views and practices were an offence to heaven and unless curtailed were a danger to the body politic. Some of the Church's finest men as well as the Emperor suspected a fundamental fallacy somewhere but came round to advocating the use of force.[2] In the circumstances it was impossible for an Emperor to find the wholly right answer.[3] In any case, the Emperor's settlement awaited the ratification and approval of a Council of bishops who represented the Church.

PRELUDE TO THE COUNCIL

After long years of bitter feud amongst Christians, the opportunity had surely now come for an oecumenical settlement. Both the Emperors were Nicene by conviction and many men of goodwill had rallied to that side.

---

[1] *Vita*, lines 1305–95.

[2] St John Chrysostom, who himself died as a result of manhandling by the state, at one time opposed coercion. Later he himself used the laws against the Arians. St Ambrose was aghast at the idea of capital punishment being used but advocated other forceful means. St Gregory Nazianzen hoped gentle treatment would bring heretics to a better mind, then asked the state to punish them. St Augustine's letter to Vincentius (*Ep.* XCIII) reminds us that it may be good to use force to prevent men from committing spiritual suicide, and to liberate them from the bad influences about them so that they may freely embrace the truth. The arguments by Christians for the use of force were first elicited by the need to deal with heresy. They were soon applied to paganism. The modern state can do much better than the Theodosian, which sometimes had to wait two generations. Now within a lifetime the convert can be an orthodox Communist, Muslim or Catholic, or what you will. See also R. H. Bainton, *The Travail of Religious Liberty*, London, 1953, and W. W. Sargant, *Battle for the Mind*, London, 1957.

[3] On this dilemma see G. Kitson Clark, *The Kingdom of Free Men*, Cambridge, 1957.

Gratian was senior Augustus and seems at one time to have envisaged a plenary council of bishops from east and west meeting at Aquileia. It is difficult to piece together in detail the circumstances in which in fact two councils met, one in the east and one in the west. Palladius of Ratiaria protested at Aquileia that his case had come before a council which was not general or plenary.[1] He had been led to expect the presence of oriental bishops, indeed the Emperor Gratian himself had said he had ordered orientals to come. St Ambrose did not deny Palladius' statement, but remarked that in earlier times a council was held in such a way that the orientals met in the east and the westerners in the west. They (the westerners) had met according to the Emperor's command at Aquileia. The easterners were free to come, but knowing the custom, did not think they ought to come. It is clear from the *Acta* that St Ambrose had a hand in getting Gratian to narrow the scope of Aquileia. Theodosius also played a part, for in his letter '*Sanctum*' St Ambrose uses words which suggest pretty plainly that Theodosius refused a general council and held a council at Constantinople.[2]

It is possible that the Emperors had intended to hold a general council but in view of the difficulties of a united meeting had decided to hold twin councils, after the manner of Constantius' Council of Ariminum and Seleucia of 359. But there is no hint in the documents of 381 that the two councils together constituted a single oecumenical council; there was no attempt to correlate their findings. We saw earlier that Theodosius was asserting the independence of the east; he sent out the letters of summons and to him the Fathers sent their concluding letter.[3] Presumably it was a council of the bishops of Theodosius' domains to which some others were invited and which later came to be accepted as oecumenical.

In some ways the result of the council was a foregone conclusion. Theodosius had already shown what he thought about people who were not Nicenes. Five months before the council met he issued a law which so closely anticipated the council's work that the great Gothofredus, without any textual evidence, considered that the date must be wrong and that the law should come after the council. The Emperor laid down that the

---

[1] *Gesta concilii Aquileiensis* 6 ff., in Ambrose's *Epp.* between *Ep.* 8 and 9 (*PL* 16 col. 916 ff.). See also Kauffmann's edition of *Dissertatio Maximini contra Ambrosium*, Strassburg, 1899, pp. 4 ff. Homes Dudden's *Life and Times of St Ambrose* and Palanque's *S. Ambroise* deal with this important council in detail so its affairs are only mentioned where they impinge on Theodosius. But see also below, pp. 46 f.

[2] *Ep.* XIII 4, see below p. 46.

[3] Socrates V 8; Theodoret V 6. The *Acta* of Constantinople 381, if there were any, have not survived. Photius himself had difficulties here, *Bibliotheca*, Codd. XV ff., XXXI (*PG* 103 col. 56 and 64). The sequence of events has to be pieced together as best we can.

heretics were to have no place to celebrate their mysteries, and that any special rescript which had been obtained by fraud on their behalf was invalid. All crowds of heretics were to be kept away from their illicit gatherings. The name of the one and supreme God was everywhere to be celebrated, and the observance of the Nicene faith, which was long ago handed down by the ancestors, and confirmed by the witness and assurance of holy religion, was to be maintained. The Photinians, the Arians and Eunomians were condemned. Then the law defined who was an upholder of this Nicene faith and a true keeper of the Catholic religion. He was one who confessed the all-powerful God, and Christ, the Son of God, under one name to be God from God, light from light; he was one who did not violate the Holy Spirit by denying him. The undivided *substantia* of the Trinity was then equated in meaning with the Greek word οὐσία. The Emperor commanded that these proven truths were to be venerated, and that those who did not respect them were to be kept away from the churches, since all heretics were forbidden to form unlawful congregations in towns. If any attempted seditions and disturbances, they were to be driven even from the walls, in order that the Catholic churches throughout the world might be restored to all the orthodox bishops who held the Nicene faith.[1]

It is clear that the Emperor was not going to tolerate deviationists on either side of the Nicene groups. The Photinians were followers of the type of teaching set forth by Marcellus of Ancyra and were much better able in their theology to grasp the oneness of the Trinity than the threeness. At the other extreme were the Eunomians, who while they agreed that the Father and the Son had much in common, insisted that it was the

---

[1] XVI : 5 : 6 of 10 January 381 to the Praetorian Prefect of the East: '*Nullus haereticis mysteriorum locus, nulla ad exercendam animi obstinatioris dementiam pateat occasio. Sciant omnes etiam si quid speciali quolibet rescripto per fraudem elicito ab huiusmodi hominum genere impetratum est, non valere. Arceantur cunctorum haereticorum ab inlicitis congregationibus turbae. Unius et summi dei nomen ubique celebretur; Nicaenae fidei dudum a maioribus traditae et divinae religionis testimonio atque adsertione firmatae observantia semper mansura teneatur; Fotinianae labis contaminatio, Arriani sacrilegii venenum, Eunomianae perfidiae crimen et nefanda monstruosis nominibus auctorum prodigia sectarum ab ipso etiam aboleantur auditu. Is autem Nicaenae adsertor fidei, catholicae religionis verus cultor accipiendus est, qui omnipotentem deum et Christum filium dei uno nomine confitetur, deum de deo, lumen ex lumine: qui spiritum sanctum, quem ex summo rerum parente speramus et accipimus, negando non violat: apud quem intemeratae fidei sensu viget incorruptae trinitatis indivisa substantia, quae Graeci adsertione verbi οὐσία recte credentibus dicitur. Haec profecto nobis magis probata, haec veneranda sunt. Qui vero isdem non inserviunt, desinant adfectatis dolis alienum verae religionis nomen adsumere et suis apertis criminibus denotentur. Ab omnium submoti ecclesiarum limine penitus arceantur, cum omnes haereticos inlicitas agere intra oppida congregationes vetemus ac, si quid eruptio factiosa temptaverit, ab ipsis etiam urbium moenibus exterminato furore propelli iubeamus, ut cunctis orthodoxis episcopis, qui Nicaenam fidem tenent, catholicae ecclesiae toto orbe reddantur.*'

admitted differences between them which were of theological significance. The Arians mentioned by the law are presumably the less extreme Arians like Demophilus and Dorotheus of Antioch.[1] The Emperor's purpose is clear. The Nicenes are to hold the cities and prosper while the others are to be driven into the oblivion of the wilderness. The churches handed over to the Nicenes were not to be replaced, for within a few months the Emperor ordered that no Eunomian or Arian or follower of Aëtius was to construct churches in city or country.[2]

The reference to *nomen summi dei* reminds us that the state religion is a continuation of the vague monotheism of Constantine's early days or for that matter of Licinius and Aurelian. It was perhaps a greater jump from the old polytheism to this than from this to Christianity. But Theodosius is no mere vague monotheist. The law carefully defines who is a Catholic with the aid of a quotation from the creed of Nicaea 325. It is difficult to say which is more remarkable, a book of Roman law laying down what Christians are to believe or a Christian Creed being quoted as higher authority by Roman law. It is noticeable that the homoousion is not brought in. The God from God theology was old and pre-Nicene, and really the basis of Cappadocian trinitarian thinking. The statement about the Holy Spirit is no more breathtaking; even an adherent of the Pneumatomachoi did not, on the face of it, violate the Holy Spirit by denying him. If he wished to state explicitly that the Spirit was a creature, presumably he denied him, but if he refrained from calling the Spirit God he would apparently fall outside the scope of this law.

One of the Nicene anathemata had equated οὐσία and ὑπόστασις. The Cappadocians had (perhaps artificially) differentiated between the two so that it became orthodox to talk of μία οὐσία and τρεῖς ὑποστάσεις, although it was heresy to talk of *tres substantiae*. The writer of the law makes it absolutely clear that *substantia* does not represent ὑπόστασις, but οὐσία. In fact, he has turned his back on the μία ὑπόστασις of Sardica and has opened the way for men to accept τρεῖς ὑποστάσεις, the watchwords of the old semi-Arians.

The great similarity with the theology and thinking of the Council of 381 will become apparent as the latter is pieced together. But the contrast between the theology of this law and that of *Cunctos populos* of February 380 is also striking. In that law, in typically 'western' style, the Father, the Son and the Spirit were confessed to be one deity under equal

---

[1] On Eunomius see especially Philostorgius IX 18 f. and X 1. (Cf. Sozomen VII 6 and Valesius at *PG* 67 col. 587 ff.) Philostorgius carefully distinguishes between Eunomians and Arians. He mentions that as a result of this law a number of bishops had to leave their sees.   [2] XVI : 5 : 8. Aëtius was one of the teachers of Eunomius.

majesty. Now in typically 'eastern' style the emphasis is on the oneness of Father and Son, while the Holy Spirit is not to be violated by denial. It is possible to suggest that in 380 Theodosius was a good westerner, but now he has come to see what is the genuine, native and 'catholic' thinking of his own domains. Perhaps he has had the good sense to see that it is a legitimate expression of the truth, and to move towards it, and the influence of Meletius is already being felt. On the other hand one must not exaggerate the difference between 'eastern' and 'western' thinking at this time.

THE COUNCIL MEETS—ITS PROCEEDINGS

The Fathers assembled in May 381 at Constantinople. Meletius, Bishop of Antioch, seems from the first to have taken the lead.[1] Theodoret tells of how in his days as Gratian's general, just before he was made Emperor, Theodosius dreamt that he was given the robe and crown by Meletius. Therefore, when the Council met, Theodosius ordered that no one should tell him who Meletius was, but he recognized him, thanks to his memory of the dream, and greeted him, and gave him great honour.[2]

This story may indicate the extent to which Theodoret was amazed by the change in the Emperor's policy towards the easterners.[3] On the other hand it is possible that Theodosius did not support Meletius from the beginning merely out of a shrewd natural hesitancy which had by this time been overcome. Certainly the Council now proceeded to carry through a Meletian programme.

One of the Bishop of Antioch's first tasks seems to have been the consecration of St Gregory Nazianzen as Bishop of Constantinople. Westerners were, later on, to object to Gregory because he had been translated from Sasima, but the easterners must have known that he was ordained by Basil to that wretched posting station under constraint, and had never taken up his work there. Originally the Emperor must have been unaware of the western view, but although there had been time for news of the western opposition to Gregory to reach him, he still had not withdrawn his support.[4]

---

[1] Socrates V 8. Gregory Nazianzen, *Vita*, lines 1514 ff.

[2] Theodoret V 6 and 7. According to Schoo (*Die Quellen des Kirchenhistorikers Sozomenos*) Theodoret may have been drawing on an Antiochene life of Meletius. The dream is not mentioned in Gregory of Nyssa's funeral oration (*PG* 46 col. 851 ff.) nor in John Chrysostom's homily on Meletius (*PG* 50 col. 515 ff.).

[3] The writer owes this comment and many another to Professor H. Chadwick, who is not however to be held responsible for their expression.

[4] Damasus, while he rejected Maximus, was against translations and therefore rejected Gregory (*Epp.* V and VI, *PL* 13 col. 365 ff.). St Ambrose accepted Maximus (*Ep.* XIII 4, *PL* 16 col. 951 f.).

Traditionally the Council of 381 consisted of 150 Holy Fathers.[1] Few westerners were present. From a contemporary's point of view it is possible to suggest that it was an eastern council to which a few westerners had been invited. The fewness would call for no comment. Similarly there was no official Papal delegate, although Ascholius had been briefed by Pope Damasus. Probably no contemporary would have commented. But for us it is significant that the decisions of a group of easterners could be accepted as oecumenical. While the Council was on, although they arrived late, the bishops from Macedonia and from Egypt seem to have upheld the western point of view.[2] There were a fair number of bishops from Palestine, and if they were led by their natural leaders, Cyril of Jerusalem and Gelasius of Caesarea, they probably supported the Meletians from Antioch, both in doctrinal and personal matters. Bishops from Antioch's sphere of influence were present in large numbers, and under their leader, Meletius, they had allied with the Cappadocians. After the death of Meletius, they were probably led by Diodore of Tarsus and Flavian. The inland areas of Asia Minor were well represented, and if the work of Basil the Great had been successful, their bishops stood for the Cappadocian theology. Their leaders were probably Amphilochius of Iconium and Helladius of Caesarea. Their theologians were Gregory of Nazianzus and Gregory of Nyssa, the greatest theologians of the day. These were the main groups present at the beginning of the Council.

Thirty-six 'Macedonians' led by Eleusius of Cyzicus and Marcian of Lampsacus, mainly from the Hellespont, also attended at first. Every step seems to have been taken to conciliate them, but they departed before long, presumably at their own desire.[3] No Arians were present, for they were already proscribed by the Emperor. One Apollinarian at least, Timothy of Berytus, was present. Laodicea was represented by Pelagius.[4] The 'Old Nicene' group at Antioch which was led by Paulinus and

---

[1] For the tradition see Socrates V 8, Sozomen VII 7, Theodoret V 7. A discussion of the bishop lists by the writer will be found in *Studia Patristica*, ed. Aland and Cross, Berlin, 1957 (vol. I, pp. 635 ff.). Opposite p. 98 a map prepared on the basis of a revised Patmian list shows the main areas represented, as well as the area conspicuous by lack of representation.

[2] For instance, Gregory Nazianzen (*Vita*, lines 1796 ff.) shows that the westerners were not only interested in opposing doctrinal aberrations, they also attacked his position as Bishop of Constantinople and agitated over the succession at Antioch. This was in keeping with the policy of Damasus and Ambrose.

[3] Socrates V 8.

[4] This Pelagius also represented Laodicea at a council held by Meletius at Antioch in 363 (Socrates III 25). It is not easy to establish Apollinarius' exact position in the episcopal succession at Laodicea, but see G. L. Prestige, *St Basil the Great and Apollinarius of Laodicea*, ed. H. Chadwick, London, 1956, pp. 13 f. It would seem that Pelagius was committed to the Meletian side while Apollinarius was in some ways an 'Old Nicene'.

was in communion with Rome was not represented, though its fate depended on the council.

All seems to have been going well at the council, when St Meletius died.[1] The council was leaderless. It has been suggested that after the death of Meletius there was inevitably a pause in the proceedings of the Council, and things only came to life again with the arrival of the Egyptians and Ascholius of Thessalonica. The implication seems to be that there were no westerners present, and that Ascholius was not invited, till Theodosius, to end the stalemate, sent an emergency summons to him. It is possible that Theodosius had refrained from calling him, at the request of Meletius, for any ecclesiastical politician would know how the presence of westerners would complicate the issues since they were hostile to Meletius.[2] Of course one's judgment is easily affected by the view one takes about whether Thessalonica was in Theodosius' Empire at this time or no.[3] But this need not be the case. There will never be any definitive answer to the problem of the divisions of Illyricum at this time, but whether Thessalonica was in the eastern or the western Empire, does not mean that east and west were sealed off from one another ecclesiastically. It was most natural that Ascholius, who had baptized Theodosius, and whose seat was geographically close to Constantinople, should be invited. Easterners were free to come to Aquileia, and there is some evidence that other westerners, or bishops of East Illyricum, were present at Constantinople. There is also good evidence that Ascholius and the bishops of Macedonia were invited, not as an afterthought, but before the council began. Pope Damasus wrote to Ascholius and the other bishops of Macedonia, in late 380 or early 381, telling them to resist contraventions of the canons against translation. He has the Council of Constantinople in mind, for he mentions it by name, and tells Ascholius to see that an irreproachable prelate is chosen as bishop. He rejects the candidature of Maximus the Cynic. It would seem then that Damasus was of the opinion that Ascholius had been invited.[4]

---

[1] Gregory Nazianzen, *Vita*, lines 1572–82. On the loss suffered by the Church at this sudden death see Gregory of Nyssa, *Oratio funebris in magnum Meletium* (*PG* 46 col. 852 ff.). [2] Schwartz, *ZNTW* XXXIV, 1935, p. 203.

[3] Illyricum was like a no-man's-land between the eastern and western centres of Roman power, now the whole of it, now the part of it, belonged to one or the other. There is not enough evidence to decide which area belonged to Theodosius at this time, though the question remains a happy hunting-ground for historian and numismatist. On the whole one suspects that Thessalonica passed out of Theodosius' hands before 381, that Palladius of Ratiaria and Secundianus were not his subjects at the time of the Council of Aquileia, and that when Valentinian II fled to Thessalonica in 387 he was not coming on to Theodosius' land.

[4] Pope Damasus, *Ep.* V (*PL* 13 col. 365 ff.). Ambrose's reference to persons unnamed (in *Ep.* XIII 7, the reference is clearly to Theodosius and his advisers, '*qui unius*

It remains to explain the absence of the Egyptians at the beginning of the council, and their late arrival with the bishops of Macedonia. Peter died and was succeeded by his brother Timothy on 14 February.[1] No new Bishop of Alexandria in those days, especially if he succeeded as a member of an ecclesiastical dynasty, could leave his seat immediately after accession. He had to secure himself against any possible attempt by the Alexandrian church to free itself from his family, and of the churches of Egypt and Libya to liberate themselves from Alexandria. It would be some time before Timothy could secure his bishopric, put his church's affairs in order, and set out on a long journey and possibly a prolonged absence. It was also natural that Ascholius would delay his arrival to coincide with that of his ecclesiastical allies, the Egyptians.

After the death of Meletius there can hardly have been much of a pause, for the matter of a successor for Meletius would immediately be raised. Some of the sources indicate there was a kind of compact by which the outstanding priests at Antioch bound themselves not to become bishop while Meletius or Paulinus lived.[2] Gregory Nazianzen however did not know of the pact. He considered that the question should never have been raised; it was obvious that the survivor should succeed. The westerners were also ignorant of any such compact, for in their letter *Sanctum* they had made the same suggestion.[3]

Theodosius did not interfere in the struggle over the succession at Antioch, though if he had been as loyal to the views of the Bishops of Alexandria and Rome as he sounded in 379, he should have prevented a new consecration. Paulinus was left in his position. In addition to him, Flavian was consecrated Bishop of Antioch. The oriental bishops, then, refused to listen to St Gregory's pleas about the succession at Antioch. The Macedonians and Egyptians attacked St Gregory on the basis of his translation to Constantinople, though they assured him they had no animosity against him personally. St Gregory longed to be away from it all, and thought, as a new Jonah, he would remove himself from their presence. He went to ask Theodosius' permission to resign. He did not declare his purpose to start with, but asked the Emperor to promise him a favour, and on this promise being made, he revealed that he wanted to retire. Theo-

---

Ascholii episcopi ita exspectandum esse putaverunt judicium, ut de Occidentalibus partibus Constantinopolim evocandum putarent'), does not suggest that Ascholius was not originally invited; the emphasis is on his summons from the west and the importance of western opinion.

[1] *Chron. Min.* I, p. 297. Schwartz, *ZNTW* XXXIV, 1935, p. 203.
[2] Socrates V 5; Sozomen VII 11; Theodoret V 3, 23. Cf. F. Cavallera, *Le Schisme d'Antioch*, pp. 232–43; R. Devreesse, *Le Patriarcat d'Antioche*.
[3] Gregory, *Vita*, lines 1573–639, Ambrose, *Ep.* XIII 2.

dosius does not seem to have been pleased, but had to keep his promise.[1] St Gregory was succeeded by Nectarius, an old man whose home was Tarsus, who had been a senator of Constantinople, and who, as Praetor, had gained popularity with the people by liberally providing games. According to Socrates he was elected by the people. Sozomen says that Nectarius called on Diodore of Tarsus when the bishops were drawing up lists of possible successors to St Gregory. Diodore decided he was the man for Constantinople, and engaged the support of the Bishop of Antioch. Nectarius was therefore placed on the list. Theodosius on perusing the list chose Nectarius, to everyone's surprise, for he was not yet even baptized. Sozomen remarks at the end of his account of the election that these facts were based on his own investigation. The following elements in Socrates' and Sozomen's accounts are trustworthy—Nectarius had popular support, he was the nominee of the 'Meletians', he received the support of the Emperor. The letter of the Synod of Constantinople of 382 to the westerners confirms this conclusion. In it the Fathers remark that during the Oecumenical Council, in the presence of Theodosius, with the consent of the clergy and people, they ordained Nectarius as Bishop of Constantinople.[2]

We can only guess at the motives of Theodosius in choosing Nectarius. No doubt the support of the oriental bishops and of the people carried some weight. Homes Dudden implies that Theodosius may have hoped he had found a second Ambrose, others suggest he wanted a cipher. But the Emperor's choice of a gentle old man, used to the ways of the city and the court, who needed to be taught his work as bishop, would indicate that he wanted peace in the Church of Constantinople. Perhaps he also wanted it to be run by one whose merits as an organizer and a showman were proved; probably he had had enough of genius in St Gregory. Above all, he had in Nectarius someone who had no ecclesiastical past. The man was a neophyte.[3]

---

[1] *Vita*, lines 1796–904. Gregory at this time preached his farewell sermon (*Or.* XLII, *Supremum Vale, PG* 36 col. 457 ff.). He says that the theological views expressed therein are those of his hearers, that is of many members of the Council. In his exposition of the faith he states there is one φύσις of the Three, God. The Father is the union from whom and to whom they flow up and back (14, 15). The Three are of the same οὐσία and glory. There is one οὐσία and a triad of hypostases, or πρόσωπα. The three are not distinguished by their natures but by their individuating characteristics (ἰδιότησιν, 16). He then speaks of him who is Unbegotten, of the Begotten and of him who proceeds. Gregory definitely uses the homoousion of the Spirit, though Basil did not do so in his *De Spiritu Sancto* nor do the Councils of 381/382 in their official documents. Gregory as a resigned archbishop was freer than a Council to state what he believed.

[2] Socrates V 8; Sozomen VII 8; cf. Gregory, *De se ipso et de episcopis*, lines 402–20. The letter will be found at Theodoret V 9.

[3] Homes Dudden, *The Life and Times of St Ambrose*, p. 212. Professor H. Chadwick kindly drew my attention to the importance of Nectarius' *tabula rasa*.

THE END OF THE COUNCIL, ITS CANONS AND ITS CREED

The Council came to an end in the middle of July. Before it dispersed, it drew up some canons, sent a synodical letter to Theodosius, and accepted a doctrinal statement which may have included a creed.

The Council promulgated four canons,[1] and although there is no evidence that Theodosius in any way affected their content, it is necessary to outline their import, since he accepted the work of the Council and was asked to implement it. The first canon orders that the faith of the 318 Fathers who met at Nicaea should not be set aside, but remain in force. Then the Fathers proceed to anathematize every heresy, especially that of the Eunomians or Anomoeans, of the Arians or Eudoxians, of the Semi-Arians or Pneumatomachoi, of the Sabellians, of the Marcellians, of the Photinians, and of the Apollinarians. The Council of 381 did not think of itself as innovating: it was establishing the faith of Nicaea. The heresies it condemns are those that had arisen since 325.[2] It is interesting to compare these anathematisms with the heresies condemned by Theodosius' laws. The teaching of all the heretics named by the canon was condemned by the law of January 381, but that law only mentioned the Eunomians, the Arians, and the Photinians by name.[3] The Sabellians are not mentioned in the Code, presumably because no heretics survived under that name. The Marcellians are not mentioned till 428, perhaps because they were included by Theodosius under the label 'Photinians'.[4] It is significant that the Pneumatomachoi and the Apollinarians were not condemned by the Emperor's laws till 383.[5] It is possible that the Emperor lagged behind the Council, in the hope of reconciling these heretics who were not far from the catholic faith.

[1] It is usually accepted that Canons V and VI belong to Constantinople 382 (see the Ballerini brothers' statement, PL 56 col. 18), and that Canon VII is not really a canon, and belongs to the fifth century. (See W. Bright, *The Canons of the First Four General Councils*, p. 120.) A letter written from Constantinople about how heretics are to be received is given in the Syriac collection of canons after the bishop list of Chalcedon. 'Canon VII' is clearly an extract from this letter. (F. Schulthess, 'Die syrischen Kanones der Synoden von Nicaea bis Chalcedon', *Abh. der königl. Gesell. der Wissen. zu Göttingen*, phil.-hist. Kl., N.F. X 2, Berlin, 1908, p. 145, MS A only.)

[2] The Sabellians are the exception. It is possible that 'the Sabellians' is a generic heading under which stand 'the Marcellians' and 'the Photinians'.

[3] XVI : 5 : 6.

[4] XVI : 5 : 65.

[5] XVI : 5 : 11 and 12. Socrates (V 9) and Sozomen (VII 10) tell us that soon after the council of 381 Theodosius brought back the remains of Paul, the Nicene bishop who was exiled and killed in the reign of Constantius at the instigation of Macedonius, the homoean Bishop of Constantinople. He placed the remains in a church whence he had ejected the Macedonians for their wrong belief. Possibly an earlier law against them has been lost, or the Emperor's legislation lagged behind his action. Cf. W. Telfer on Paul of Constantinople in *HTR* XLIII, 1950, pp. 31 ff.

The second canon orders bishops not to go outside their diocese into churches beyond their boundaries, and cause confusion; but, according to the canons, the Bishop of Alexandria shall administer the affairs of Egypt only; the bishops of the orient shall have charge of the orient only, while safeguarding the seniority of the church of Antioch, as laid down in the Canons of Nicaea; similarly the bishops of the Diocese of Asia shall administer the affairs of Asia only, and those of Pontica the affairs of Pontica only, and those of Thracia the affairs of Thracia only. Unless invited, no bishop shall go beyond his diocese for an ordination or any other ecclesiastical administration. While safeguarding the canon which has been written before regarding dioceses, it is manifest that in each province the provincial synod shall rule according to what was laid down in Nicaea. But it is necessary that the churches of God among the barbarians (that is outside the imperial frontiers) be administered according to the custom of the Fathers.[1]

In this canon 'diocese' is used in the sense it bears in imperial civil administration, that is, it means a group of provinces. At Nicaea the Church had thought in terms of provinces, and had set up provincial councils, to deal with the affairs of the province (Canons IV and V). At the Council of Antioch, the Church ratified this arrangement and brought the Metropolitans into greater prominence.[2] The Council of 381 thinks in terms of the great diocesan areas, but it makes no provision for a machinery which is over all the dioceses. They are, it would seem to be, autocephalous; orthodoxy of faith, it may be presumed, is their bond of unity. It may be said that it is a tragedy that the Council did not set up some machinery for the regular calling of Oecumenical Councils. This would have provided a supreme court of appeal, so preventing ecclesiastical tyranny within the dioceses; it might have prevented the great bishops from competing with one another for primacy, but this is to ask too much of the Fathers of 381.

The third canon lays down that the Bishop of Constantinople shall have a seniority of honour after the Bishop of Rome, for it is a new Rome.[3] This canon really grants nothing by way of material advantage to Con-

---

[1] On interference by bishops outside their own area see Hamilton Hess, *The Canons of the Council of Sardica*, Oxford, 1958, pp. 80 ff.; K. Lübeck, *Reichseinteilung und Kirchliche Hierarchie des Orients*, Münster, 1901, pp. 172–91, and Müller in *Festgabe Jülicher*, Tübingen, 1927. On churches outside the Empire see C. H. Turner, *Studies in Early Church History*, Oxford, 1912, pp. 46 f.

[2] Canons XII and XIV. Probably they belonged to Antioch 329, but were collected under Antioch 341.

[3] Cf. Socrates I 16 and Sozomen II 3. A discussion of this Canon is included in every work on the position of the Papacy, so little need be said.

stantinople, while it explicitly recognizes the primacy of honour held by the see of Rome. Alexandria had always claimed the second place and no doubt this canon did little to improve relationships. Antioch and Jerusalem, which had superlative claims to be the original apostolic seats of Christianity, seem to have made no protest during these years against the rise of Constantinople. Ephesus, which could claim both St Paul and St John, would probably be the most severely affected. So far as Theodosius is concerned, he remained on good terms with the see of Rome, and he respected the rights and privileges of other churches. He did nothing, so far as we know, to press the rights of the church of Constantinople. Nonetheless, from this time onwards, the eminence of the Bishops of Constantinople increased.[1]

In the fourth canon the Fathers deny that Maximus the Cynic is, or was, a bishop, and declare invalid his ordinations and actions. Theodosius had already rejected Maximus, and Pope Damasus had done the same.[2] St Ambrose indeed was supporting him about this time but seems to have dropped his candidature for the seat of Constantinople within a year, for the matter was not raised at the synod of Rome in 382.

The evidence connecting the Niceno-Constantinopolitan creed in some way with the Council of 381 is so overwhelmingly strong that it makes it difficult not to consider that creed an integral part of the Theodosian settlement.[3] It is necessary therefore to say something briefly on some points of its theology.[4] In the first place C is as firm about the *homoousion* of the Son as N.[5] The Arians are definitely shut out. Similarly if the clause 'whose Kingdom shall have no end' is meant to imply there will be no retraction of the Trinity, the men of the opposite extreme, the followers of Marcellus and Photinus, are excluded. The Creed does not attribute the *homoousion* to the Spirit; there is still a conciliatory gap left

---

[1] As an example one may cite the Synod held in 394 under the presidency of Nectarius while Theodosius was in the west. Bagadius of Bostra appealed to Rome against his deposition, but the case was settled by an eastern synod sitting under the Bishop of Constantinople. (L. Duchesne, *Églises séparées*, Paris, 1896, pp. 203 f.; Hefele-Leclerq II 1, 97 f.)

[2] *Ep.* V, *PL* 13 col. 365, dated in Jaffé-Wattenbach (*Regesta Pontificum Romanorum* I, Leipzig, 1888, p. 38) to 380.

[3] The case is stated in J. N. D. Kelly, *Early Christian Creeds*, pp. 296 ff. See also Appendix A. It is useful to use Dr Kelly's abbreviations—N for the Creed of 325 and C for the Niceno-Constantinopolitan.

[4] N and C are two distinct documents and so a phrase missing here or there does not mean a change of theological intent.

[5] Harnack's sneer that the Fathers of 381 played a practical joke on the Church and understood ὁμοούσιος in the sense of ὁμοιούσιος (*Dogmengeschichte*, 4th ed., II, pp. 276 f.) cannot withstand the detailed argumentation of Bethune-Baker (*The Meaning of Homoousios in the Constantinopolitan Creed*, Cambridge, 1905) and G. L. Prestige (*God in Patristic Thought*, 2nd ed., London, 1952).

open for the Pneumatomachoi. It is likely that the Apollinarians were not excluded.[1] These omissions are all the more remarkable in that the westerners had condemned both those who contended against the Spirit and those who denied a human highest faculty in the Incarnate. The Creed sets forth the catholic faith in its main essentials in terms of breathtaking majesty and liturgical beauty. By lending his support to such a statement of faith, Theodosius was doing much to ensure the permanence of the settlement to which he was trying to bring the Church.[2]

The Council sent a letter to Theodosius before it broke up, giving thanks to God and to the Emperor. The Fathers said that they had met in accordance with Theodosius' letters and had brought themselves to harmony. They had confirmed the faith of Nicaea by 'summary definitions' (συντομούς ὅρους), and anathematized the heresies which had contended against it. They had promulgated canons relating to the good order of the Church. They requested that their findings be given the force of law.[3]

The Emperor responded to the letter of the Council with *Episcopis tradi* of 30 July 381. He ordered that all the churches were to be immediately handed over to the bishops who confessed that the Father, the Son and the Holy Spirit were of one majesty and power, of the same glory, of one splendour, who did nothing out of harmony by introducing profane division, but who upheld the order of the Trinity by asserting the persons and the unity of the divinity. These were the bishops who were in communion with Nectarius Bishop of the church of Constantinople, those who in Egypt were in communion with Timothy of Alexandria; those who in the parts of the east were in communion with Pelagius Bishop of Laodicea and Diodore of Tarsus; those who in proconsular Asia and the Asiatic Diocese were in communion with Amphilochius of Iconium and Optimus of Antioch,[4] those who in the Pontic diocese were in communion with Helladius of Caesarea and Otreius of Melitene, and Gregory of Nyssa . . . (and those who were in communion with)[5] Terennius Bishop of (Tomi in) Scythia, and Marmarius Bishop of

---

[1] The phrase 'from Holy Spirit and Mary the Virgin' has been taken since ancient times to have an anti-Apollinarian intent (Kelly, *Creeds*, p. 333), but it does not very explicitly contradict their basic tenet that the incarnate Lord did not have a human highest faculty. Ultimately and logically of course birth from a human woman implies a complete humanity.

[2] We have Theodosius partly to thank for 'one of the few threads by which the tattered fragments of the divided robe of Christendom are held together' (Kelly, quoted in his preface by J. Burnaby, *The Belief of Christendom*, London, 1959).

[3] Mansi col. 557; Sozomen VII 9.   [4] Antioch in Pisidia.

[5] The text of the Code does not give evidence of a break here or of a repetition, but a break must have occurred for the bishops then named cannot be classed as Pontic.

Marcianopolis. These must be admitted to the tenure of catholic churches as a result of communion and alliance with worthy bishops. All those moreover who dissented in communion of faith from those whom the special detail had set forth (that is, the list of bishops above) were to be expelled from the churches as manifest heretics. Nor from henceforth was any power or facility to be allowed them of obtaining control of the churches, in order that the priesthood of the true and Nicene faith might persist in purity. After the publication of the form of this order, no place was to be given to malignant deceit.[1]

The law begins with a theological statement. The Father, the Son and the Holy Spirit are declared to be one in majesty, power, glory, splendour and divinity, but within the Trinity there is an order, dispensation, of *personae*. It is striking that the Holy Three are not said to be 'of one substance'. The author of the law can hardly be afraid to ascribe the homoousion to the Son, so probably it is with reference to the Holy Spirit that the law is being cautious. This is thoroughly in keeping with the official theology of the Cappadocians and of the dominant party at the Council.

The list of leading bishops given by the law is most illuminating. The Bishop of Rome is presumably not named because the law deals with the eastern part of the Empire. The contrast with *Cunctos populos* of February 380 is nonetheless apparent. The Bishop of Constantinople is placed first. Already the third canon is having its effect in official circles. No bishop of Antioch on the Orontes is named, probably to avoid making an official ruling in the dispute between Flavian and Paulinus.[2] We may say in conclusion with regard to this law, that Theodosius has settled down both in the matter of doctrine and of persons to a policy which strongly

[1] XVI : 1 : 3 to Auxonius, Proconsul of Asia. '*Episcopis tradi omnes ecclesias mox iubemus, qui unius maiestatis adque virtutis patrem et filium et spiritum sanctum confitentur eiusdem gloriae, claritatis unius, nihil dissonum profana divisione facientes, sed trinitatis ordinem personarum adsertione et divinitatis unitate, quos constabit communioni Nectari episc(opi) Constantinopolitanae ecclesiae nec non Timothei intra Aegyptum Alexandrinae urbis episcopi esse sociatos; quos etiam in Orientis partibus Pelagio episcopo Laodicensi et Diodoro episcopo Tarsensi : in Asia nec non proconsulari adque Asiana dioecesi Amphilochio episcopo Iconiensi et Optimo episcopo Antiocheno : in Pontica dioecesi Helladio episc(opo) Caesariensi et Otreio Meliteno et Gregorio episc(opo) Nysseno, Terennio episc(opo) Scythiae, Marmario episc(opo) Marcianop(olitano) communicare constiterit. Hos ad optinendas catholicas ecclesias ex communione et consortio probabilium sacerdotum oportebit admitti : omnes autem, qui ab eorum, quos commemoratio specialis expressit, fidei communione dissentiunt, ut manifestos haereticos ab ecclesiis expelli neque his penitus posthac obtinendarum ecclesiarum pontificium facultatemque permitti, ut verae ac Nicaenae fidei sacerdotia casta permaneant nec post evidentem praecepti nostri formam malignae locus detur astutiae.*'
[2] Despite Socrates (V 8), it is clear that the Emperor is not setting up patriarchates. Villages like Nyssa were hardly suitable. Rather, he is providing an immediate touchstone of orthodoxy.

supports the ideas of the Cappadocians and Antiochene Meletians as ratified by the Council of 381.

THE NEGOTIATIONS WITH THE WEST AND THE COUNCILS OF 382

Negotiations to end the schism between east and west had gone on for nearly a generation and no less persons than Basil, Athanasius and Ambrose had been actively engaged therein. Theodosius was by now deeply involved. The western Fathers assembled at Aquileia by the command of Gratian, having dealt with the cases of Palladius and Secundianus and secured the west against Arianism, turned their attention to the east. Led by St Ambrose they wrote the letter *Quamlibet* to Theodosius.[1] They give thanks for the benefits given by the Emperors, especially that the churches have been restored to the Catholics and the Arians removed. They regret that there is still dissension amongst the Catholics. Men who had always been in their communion (presumably they are referring to Paulinus of Antioch and men like him), have been troubled by those who hesitated in faith in days gone by (presumably, they mean men like Meletius). But for the public disorders they would have sent representatives to the east to clear matters up, but now they beg the Emperors to see to it that when one dies, the church should go to the survivor. They request a council be called to meet at Alexandria.

By the time the letter arrived it was too late for Theodosius to do anything about it. In their next letter *Sanctum* (*Ep.* XIII), St Ambrose and his colleagues say they have heard that though Meletius was dead, a candidate other than Paulinus had been intruded. Also they find it impossible to accept the consecration of Nectarius to Constantinople, the claim of Maximus (the Cynic) to that chair must be heard. They suggest a general council ought to be held. They explicitly state that Gratian told them to write.[2]

Unfortunately Theodosius' reply is lost. We may presume its contents

---

[1] Exact dating of the affairs of the Council is difficult. Judging from the internal evidence in the material which has come down to us, it looks as if the Council met in full session at midsummer 381 and this letter was written at about that time. *Ep* XIII was written soon afterwards but by now news had arrived of the death of Meletius and of the election of Flavian and Nectarius. Time must then be allowed between *Epp.* XIII and XIV for the former to reach Theodosius and his reply to come. *Ep.* XIV must therefore be placed in the autumn. Neither council, while it was in session, knew of the proceedings of the other.

[2] Maximus presented a work to Gratian (Jerome, *Viris illustr.* CXXVII) and may have ingratiated himself thereby. Maximus had not deceived the politic Damasus (*Epp.* V and VI: *PL* 13 col. 365 ff.). The Pope seems to have recognized Nectarius as Bishop of Constantinople in 381 (Duchesne, *Églises séparées*, p. 268).

from *Fidei* (*Ep.* XIV). Ambrose and his friends deny that they go in for fable-mongering and prattle. They do not want to interfere with anybody, but they are anxious because of the break in communion. They are not only concerned with the people about whom Theodosius wrote (presumably Flavian and Nectarius) but about the teaching of Apollinarius. An inquiry should be made in the presence of the parties concerned and a person who is then convicted of innovation should lay down his office and title as bishop. It is interesting to note that Theodosius did not deprive Apollinarian bishops till 388.[1] He did not send his bishops to a council in the west but in 382 a council met in his capital.

Not a great deal is known of this council. Theodoret, after he has described the work of the Fathers at Constantinople in 381, says that the next summer most of them gathered at the same place, and received a synodical letter from the bishops of the west, asking them to come to Rome, as a great synod was gathering there.[2] In their reply the easterners excused themselves from going to Rome but said they were sending a delegation with their letter and its statement of faith. They asserted their belief in the one Godhead in three hypostases. They rejected the Sabellians, the Arians, the Pneumatomachoi by name and the teaching of the Apollinarians. These were the headings of the faith they preached, but if the westerners wished to be more fully informed they could read the τόμος set forth by the Synod of Antioch and that by the oecumenical synod the year before, at Constantinople.

The close similarity between the theology upheld by the Emperor and that of this council is as apparent as the near identity of the heretics condemned by Emperor and council. Their acceptance of Nectarius at Constantinople and Cyril at Jerusalem, despite the west's disapproval, was also in accordance with his declared policy. Their recognition of Flavian at Antioch, which was in flagrant violation of the western opinion, had received Theodosius' acquiescence. It is difficult to tell whether the Emperor is dictating to the council or the council to the Emperor. Probably the two are working hand and glove.

It is clear that the eastern bishops were making overtures for reunion on the basis of a common Trinitarian and Christological faith, and that certain other matters connected with persons were being left for time to solve. Actually, with the exception in the case of Antioch, the western Church seems before very long to have been in full communion with the

[1] XVI : 5 : 14.
[2] Theodoret V 8. The synodical letter of the orientals is given at V 9.

eastern, and even the exception was received within a lifetime.[1] This could not have been achieved if the easterners had been inflexible, nor if they had given in to the west, nor without the steady support and co-operation of the Emperor.[2]

Also during the summer of 382 a Council met at Rome under Pope Damasus. Ambrose, Britton of Trèves, Ascholius of Thessalonica and Anemius of Sirmium were there. From the east there came St Jerome, Epiphanius of Salamis, Paulinus of Antioch and the three delegates sent by Constantinople 382. Apollinarianism was condemned. Paulinus was accepted as Bishop of Antioch, and communion was withdrawn from Diodore of Tarsus and Acacius of Beroea, the consecrators of Flavian.[3] Pope Damasus promulgated a most important statement on the position of the Papacy to the effect that the position of the Roman Church did not depend on the statement of Synods, but on the *Tu es Petrus* and on the Roman martyrdom of St Peter and St Paul. Alexandria owed its second place to the fact that Mark was Peter's disciple. Antioch owed its position as third to the fact that Peter had his seat there, and there the name Christian was first used.[4] It is probable that this was the Roman reaction to the third canon of the Council of 381.

Clearly a good deal still divided west and east but it was possible now to resume communion. In closing this discussion of the catholic and

[1] In 388 Paulinus died after uncanonically consecrating a successor who was recognized by the west. Theodosius twice tried to get Flavian to appear before a western synod, but did not otherwise interfere. The Council of Capua (winter 391–2) referred the matter to Theophilus of Alexandria. In 393 the Council of Caesarea recognized Flavian and the west too accepted him eventually. (Theodoret V 23, Ambrose, *Ep.* LVI, Sozomen VII 11, Socrates V 15 f.; Carthage 397 Canon XLVIII; *The Sixth Book of the Select Letters of Severus*, ed. and trans. E. W. Brooks, II 1, London, 1904, p. 223; Cavallera, *Le Schisme*, pp. 270, 283 ff.; Palanque, *Ambroise*, p. 542; Hefele-Leclerq, II 1, pp. 80 ff.; Schwartz *ZNTW* XXXIV, 1935, p. 211; Greenslade *JTS* XLVI, 1945, pp. 17 ff.)

[2] The council of 382 promulgated two canons which are usually given as V and VI of 381. In the former the Fathers say that concerning the tome of the westerners (probably the statement of Damasus' synod of 369 accepted at Antioch 379) they also receive those in Antioch who confess the godhead of the Father and the Son and the Holy Spirit to be one. The Fathers are clearly extending the hand of friendship to Paulinus and his followers at Antioch. Canon VI safeguards bishops against ecclesiastical charges by heretics.

[3] Theodoret V 9; Jerome, *Ep.* CVIII 6 (*PL* 22 col. 881); Sozomen VII 11. Palanque, *Histoire*, p. 295; *Ambroise*, pp. 102 f.; Homes Dudden, *The Life and Times of St Ambrose*, pp. 215 f.; Hefele-Leclerq II 1, p. 58.

[4] C. H. Turner, 'Latin Lists of the Canonical Books No. 1—The Roman Council under Damasus, 382' in *JTS* I, 1900, pp. 554 ff. Cf. Jalland, *The Church and the Papacy*, p. 255. The doctrinal views of Pope Damasus at about this time are set forth in his Confession sent to Paulinus (A. Hahn, *Bibliothek der Symbole*, Breslau, 1897, p. 271; cf. Theodoret V 10 f.). The Pope sets forth a pure Nicene Creed and after '*et Spiritum Sanctum*' he adds '*neque facturam, neque creaturam, sed de substantia deitatis*'. The twenty-four attached anathemata attack the same deviationists as Theodosius and the easterners. In addition he spoke out strongly against episcopal translation.

oecumenical settlement of 381/382 it remains to say that it was the only one of the settlements associated with the first four Oecumenical Councils which did not lead on to years of doctrinal strife. This was partly because it came at the end of a period of struggle and the Church was exhausted. St Jerome said of Constantius' settlement that the world awoke and groaned to find itself Arian. We hear few groans when the world finds itself Nicene in 382, perhaps because the groaners have been effectively driven out of earshot. On the other hand it may be fairer to say that Theodosius had carefully prepared for the councils, and steadily supported their decisions. The work of mutual explanation and clearing up of misunderstanding by churchmen of good will on both sides had had sufficient success for Theodosius to be able to pick out and enforce a solution which met the approval of the broad consensus of Christian opinion. In a sense he was completing and crowning the work of Athanasius and Basil.

D

3

Against all the Heresies

Cunctos populos taught us something of Theodosius' mind. For him there was one true religious law infallibly revealed by God to his authorized representatives and exhaustively laid down in Holy Scripture. Anyone who did not accept that law forfeited his rights and ought to be punished by the state. In such schemes of thought, once orthodoxy has been laid down, logically all deviationists and nonconformists will inevitably come to the government's indoctrination chamber. Only calculated postponement till a better opportunity presents itself will delay the re-education of them all. In Theodosius' case it meant that not only Christians who persisted in non-Nicene views, but pagans, Jews, Manichaeans and apostates would all have to receive treatment. Luckily few human beings logically and persistently follow up their moments of insight. The meeting of opposition also sometimes calls for reconsideration. Here Theodosius was no exception. The logic of his thought was not applied to the Jews, despite the pressure Ambrose brought to bear on him.[1] The purest specimens in our collection are Theodosius' treatment of the Manichaeans and apostates.

Since the days when the arch-persecutor Diocletian had received the co-operation of Christian bishops against the Manichaeans, the Church and the Roman state had been consistent in their hostility to that religion which had come into the Roman domains from the Persian Empire. The Persian Kings did not try to protect the Manichaeans in the Roman Empire, so though they were saved the embarrassment of the kind of support Christians in the Persian Empire received, they were without protection of any kind. As quislings with foreign connections they had forfeited the protection Roman citizen rights afforded.

In 372 Valentinian I prohibited Manichaean assemblies and ordered

---

[1] On his policy towards the Jews see Appendix D.

the confiscation of the property where such teaching had gone on.[1] In 381 in a law with effect retrospective to the previous enactment, Theodosius ordered that no Manichaean of either sex was to bequeath or inherit.[2] The Emperor removed from these people the right of testation and of living under Roman citizen rights and tried to prevent them from sheltering under other names. A year later Theodosius returned to the attack.[3] Any Manichee who under the pretence of living the solitary life avoided the society of decent people and chose that of the worst men in secret, was to lose testatory rights. But Encratitae, Saccofori and Hydroparastatae were to suffer the death penalty.[4] Inquisitors were to be appointed and informers received. Their meetings were to be forbidden. People who did not assemble together on the day of the Pascha were indubitably to be considered such as those condemned by this law.

Half-way through this law the legislator seems to have lost his head. This is the first time the death penalty was laid down for wrong belief. The hateful principle of inquisitor and informer was now also introduced to church affairs when men already viewed it as a shameful thing in other walks of life. When in a few years' time Maximus, the western usurper, put Priscillian to death and confiscated his goods, it is possible that the man was condemned as a heretic. In a letter Maximus equated Priscillianism with Manichaeism and this may be a direct reference to the law we are studying.[5]

Within four years of his accession Theodosius had reached the climax of his ferocious laws against the Manichaeans.[6] It is true that such laws had little effect on the heretics, rather they were valuable to the Emperor as manifestos before God that he was doing his best to put down names hateful to heaven.[7] No one raised his voice against the fundamental

[1] XVI : 5 : 3. [2] XVI : 5 : 7. [3] XVI : 5 : 9.
[4] These, together with the Apotactitae, were mentioned in the previous law. See also Epiphanius, Panarion XLVII, LX 1 and LIX 1 in Holl's edition with its valuable references to Irenaeus and Hippolytus. Cf. Basil, PG 32 col. 664 and 729 f. and the article 'Ascodrutae' in RAC. Their peculiarities hardly justify 'the utmost punishment and inexplicable penalty', presumably death, which was to fall on them. In contrast, the Tascodrogitae were not to be driven from their own places, but crowds were not to be allowed to gather at any of their churches (XVI : 5 : 10 of 383; cf. 65 of 428).
[5] Collectio Avellana XL. Professor S. L. Greenslade pointed out to the writer that it is probable that technically Priscillian was executed for the maleficium revealed while the alleged Manichaeism was being investigated. On Priscillian see also p. 63. It is possible that the medieval and reformation Inquisitions go back in idea to Theodosius.
[6] Some additions were made to their miseries. Their name was slipped into a 'portmanteau' law of 383 which was giving a summary of previous legislation. Presumably this added the penalties against other heretics to the particular disabilities from which they already suffered (XVI : 5 : 11; cf. XVI : 7 : 3 by Gratian). While in Rome in 389 Theodosius applied his previous measures to the west (XVI : 5 : 18).
[7] Laws against the Manichaeans and other heretics appeared with monotonous regularity. Gothofredus thinks XVI : 5 : 20 is against the Manichaeans; if so, Theo-

attack they made on human freedom; perhaps people thought Mani-chaeans after all were hardly citizens. But freedom is indivisible; the other attacks were nearer home.

In 381 Theodosius ordered that those who from being Christians became pagans, should lose the power and right of testation. In such circumstances, every testament of a dead person was to be rescinded.[1] In a law issued two years later he carefully distinguished between catechumens and the faithful. If fully initiated Christians lapsed they were to be outside the Roman law and lose the right of testamentary disposition. The same sort of rule was to apply in the matter of receiving legacies.[2]

It was not till 391 that he again turned his attention to apostates.[3] He seems not to be threatening them but to be pointing out that those who betray the faith and profane baptism through that fact become separated from all. They could not testify as witnesses and as previously enacted they could have no power of making testamentary disposition, or to inherit. Repentance and excuses could not cover pollution of the faith and betrayal of divine mysteries, so that they could never return to their earlier status. Help could be given to the lapsed and the erring, but for the lost, that is to those who profane holy baptism, there can be no remedy of penitence. In the same way, such people forfeit any splendour of rank they have either achieved or inherited.

His baptism in 380 had meant much to Theodosius. His mass murder at Thessalonica ten years later had been remedied by penance. But, says he, apostasy cannot be forgiven. This rigorist attitude suggests he had much in common with the Novatianists and Luciferians.[4] On the other hand, the dominical saying about there being no forgiveness for sin against the Holy Spirit may be in the background. Profanation of baptism could, without much stretching of the imagination, be interpreted as such a sin. One may also call to Theodosius' defence the saying that a lapsed

dosius himself had to repeat some of his measures against them. Augustine's friends at Rome seemed to have suffered nothing at the hands of the state (*Confessions* V. x). Professor S. L. Greenslade pointed out to the writer that some of this legislation may have been for propaganda purposes and was never fully enforced. This seems more than probable and we must accordingly be on our guard against thinking that coercion was always as consistent and extreme as the laws would have us believe.

[1] XVI : 7 : 1.

[2] XVI : 7 : 2. The distinction was recognized in canon law, for instance in the eleventh and fourteenth canons of Nicaea. Cf. XVI : 7 : 3 by Gratian which is closely related to this law in date.

[3] XVI : 7 : 4 and 5 are probably extracts from the same law.

[4] Compare the normal church teaching of this time as exemplified by St Ambrose, *De poenitentia*, *PL* 16 col. 465 ff., especially Bk 1 III.10, X.45 f., XI.51; Bk 2 II.6 ff., IV.27. Professor S. L. Greenslade, while admitting the difficulty of interpreting the law, points out that Theodosius was dealing with civil status while Ambrose was dealing with communion.

post-Christian is no more a simple pagan than a divorced woman is a virgin.

Legislation against apostasy to paganism was a new departure initiated by Theodosius. Such laws were not produced out of reaction to a resurgence of the old religion, for if they had been, they would have appeared during the pagan renaissance of 393 and 394. Rather, as the laws themselves reveal, they are the product of the logic of the Emperor's thinking. Christianity and Roman citizenship are to him coterminous. Someone who turns his back on Christianity forfeits his rights. A man who betrays the Empire cannot be forgiven, nor can one who rejects Christ. The laws are not so much punishing an offence as recognizing that the apostate has by his own action outlawed himself.[1]

ARIANS, PNEUMATOMACHOI AND OTHERS

Because these heretics were numerous and powerful, and therefore potentially dangerous, and because doubts entered even Theodosius' head, the Emperor's ways here will be found to be rather devious.

The Emperor had declared resoundingly for the Nicene beliefs and against heretics. He had harried them from the churches, given them no place to celebrate their mysteries, denied them the power to build new churches. Yet Theodosius was not a man incapable of reconsidering his own policies. In the spring of 383 he called a synod of all the heresies.[2] When the Arians had been turned out of the places of prayer there had been disturbances and Theodosius did not wish the cities to be filled with commotion. His qualms were not then based on anything higher than the realization that his treatment of the heretics was making impossible his duty as a Roman magistrate to maintain civil peace. But even now there was a chance that he might consider that free discussion and agreement was a way more in keeping with the genius of the Church.

Nectarius and Agelius (the Novatianist) represented the Nicenes, Demophilus the Arians, Eunomius his own people and Eleusius of Cyzicus the Macedonians. By the time the synod met in June Theodosius' old advisers had regained control and the colloquy was turned

---

[1] G. Bardy, *La Conversion au Christianisme*, Paris, 1949, has an important chapter on apostasy. The treatment of apostasy raises many problems. A young Pakistani keen on the principles of an Islamic republic pointed out to the writer that in Spain people baptized as infants into Christianity of a particular type find themselves in difficulties if they wish as adults to dissociate themselves. The punishment of apostates in Islam, based on thinking similar to that of Theodosius, still continues in some countries.

[2] Socrates V 10; Sozomen VII 12. Cf. Gregory Nazianzen, *Ep.* CLXXIII (*PG* 37 col. 281).

into a comedy.[1] The only people to benefit were the Novatianists whose doctrinal affinity to the Nicenes was accepted. Theodosius seems to have had some predilection for this type of schismatic, for during these years he showed favour also to the Luciferians who had vilified the Pope. He supported them strongly, saying they were Catholics who had maintained the faith they had received.[2]

For the rest, the juggernaut of Theodosian policy went grinding on its way. Before long the Pneumatomachoi and Macedonians, men defective in their doctrine of the Holy Spirit, were added to the list of accredited heretics. Heretics were now not to use private buildings for worship and all good men were asked to co-operate in driving them out.[3] This no doubt was as good an invitation to a pogrom as a government can give. By the end of the year the Apollinarians, who were defective in their teaching about the person of Christ, joined the ranks of the condemned.[4] The tedious repetition of previous measures and the threats against local officials which now begin to appear in the Code, indicate the effectiveness of the legislation. An attack was also launched on heretical clergy and teachers.[5] Like Septimius Severus and Decius before him, Theodosius was aiming by such measures as this to leave his opponents leaderless.

After the spring of 384 there was a slackening off of this kind of legislation. Perhaps the Emperor had gone as far as he wanted, and was succumbing to the sloth of Court life. Perhaps Flaccilla was able to exert less pressure on behalf of orthodoxy while she was carrying Honorius, who was born in September 384. After his birth she may not have quite recovered her health.[6] Flaccilla that 'soul faithful to God' died in 385.[7] The laws of 384 indicate that Theodosius travelled to the west for a

---

[1] Free discussion did not take place but each group submitted a creed. The Emperor rejected all except the Nicene faith. Sozomen (VII 6, cf. Philostorgius X 6) tells us that once when Theodosius was about to hear Eunomius, Flaccilla kept him away. This may refer to the colloquy.

[2] *Libellus precum ad imperatores* (*Collectio Avellana* II: *CSEL* XXXV; *PL* 13 col. 81 ff.). It is difficult not to doubt the genuineness of these letters.

[3] XVI : 5 : 11 to the Praetorian Prefect of the East.

[4] XVI : 5 : 12 to the same. Their inclusion was probably the result of Gregory Nazianzen's *Ep.* CXXV (*PG* 37 col. 217 ff.).

[5] XVI : 5 : 13 of 21 January 384.

[6] Gregory of Nyssa (*In funere Flacillae, PG* 46 col. 877 ff.) gives the impression that she had been ill some time before her death.

[7] The title is from Ambrose, *De obitu Theodosii* 40. Marcellinus Comes (*Chron. Min.* II p. 62) rightly dates Galla's coming to Constantinople as Theodosius' wife to 386. Presumably in accordance with his law (III : 8 : 1), he had waited a year before remarriage. Claudian (*IV cons. Honor.* 157) and Zosimus (IV 43 f.) are not reliable chronological guides. Cf. Seeck, *Regesten*, p. 273;*Gesch.*, pp. 210, 521. It is clear from Gregory of Nyssa's funeral oration that Flaccilla had contributed not a little to her husband's policy, especially in patronage of the Catholic church. See also Sozomen VII 6; Theodoret V 18; Themistius, *Or.* XIX (p. 231) and XVII (p. 225).

short time; presumably he went to Italy to discuss the situation with regard to Maximus. Perhaps the Arian Justina insisted on a milder attitude to her co-religionists as the price of her support. A little before Flaccilla died, Theodosius lost his young daughter Pulcheria.[1] Death indeed was taking a heavy toll of Theodosius' old associates. Ascholius had died in the winter of 382/3. In 384 the redoubtable and diplomatic Damasus joined his illustrious predecessors. The Emperors confirmed the election of Pope Siricius so that no serious rival contested his position.[2] In the August of 383 the newly married Emperor Gratian, fleeing before his enemies, was told his wife was at Lugdunum. He hurried thither to be treacherously murdered.[3] The strongly Nicene Gratian's death made little direct difference to Theodosius except that he was now able to assert some sort of guardianship over the young Valentinian II who was nominally ruling Italy. The real ruler was the lad's mother, Justina, and she was an Arian.

Despite all the fulminations in the Code, the Arians in the east had their places of prayer and assembly as well as their own bishops and clergy.[4] So far as the legal situation was concerned they might well have taken new heart in 385 for two laws were issued which appear to deal with toleration for them. The first was from Milan and it therefore presumably emanated from the *scrinia* of Valentinian II.[5] The Emperors gave opportunity for meeting together[6] to those who agreed with the views put forward in the time of Constantius of divine memory when the bishops were assembled from the whole Roman world and the faith was expounded at the Council of Ariminum by the very people who are recognized as dissenters. These views were confirmed by the Council of Constantinople and it was decreed they should remain in force for ever.

[1] See Gregory of Nyssa, *Oratio consolatoria in funere Pulcheriae, PG* 46 col. 863 ff.
[2] Rauschen p. 197; *Collectio Avellana* IV.
[3] It has been suggested Theodosius was somehow implicated; see Ambrose, *In psall.* LXI 25 (*PL* 14 col. 1177), Pacatus XXIV and Solari, 'L'alibi di Theodosio', *Klio* N.F. IX, 1934, pp. 165 ff. In the nature of the case it is unlikely that evidence would survive. Gaul was a long way from Constantinople and the suggestion is a needless smirch on Theodosius' character.
[4] Socrates V 23.
[5] XVI : 1 : 4: '*Damus copiam colligendi his, qui secundum ea sentiunt, quae temporibus divae memoriae Constanti sacerdotibus convocatis ex omni orbe Romano expositaque fide ab his ipsis, qui dissentire noscuntur, Ariminensi concilio, Constantinopol(itano) etiam confirmata in aeternum mansura decreta sunt. Conveniendi etiam quibus iussimus patescat arbitrium, scituris his, qui sibi tantum existimant colligendi copiam contributam, quod, si turbulentum quippiam contra nostrae tranquillitatis praeceptum faciendum esse temptaverint, ut seditionis auctores pacisque turbatae ecclesiae, etiam maiestatis capite ac sanguine sint supplicia luituri, manente nihilo minus eos supplicio, qui contra hanc dispositionem nostram obreptive aut clanculo supplicare temptaverint.*'
[6] '*Copiam colligendi*' could refer to the exacting of monetary contributions, but the meaning given is supported by Sozomen VII 13.

The right of meeting was also to be open to those named in the Emperor's command, provided that it was recognized by those who thought that to them alone opportunity for meeting had been granted, that if they did anything by way of disturbance against the precept of the Imperial Tranquillity, they would pay the penalty of treason with their head and blood as authors of sedition and disturbers of the peace of the Church. This penalty no less awaited those who tried to supplicate against this, the Emperor's disposition, stealthily or secretly.[1]

The interpretation of this law depends on which decisions of Ariminum and Constantinople are in question. It is true that the first decision of the western bishops at Ariminum in 359 pointed in a 'Nicene' direction and that this was confirmed by Constantinople 381 in the sense that the latter council confirmed previous movements towards the truth of Nicaea. But this identification of the councils does little justice to the Latin of the law which indicates that the decisions were taken in the reign of Constantius (*ob.* 361) and it contradicts the known Arian tendencies of the religious policy of Valentinian II at this time under the influence of his mother Justina. Much better sense is yielded if we admit that the *Ariminense* referred to is the final Arianizing policy imposed by Constantius II on that Council and confirmed by his Council of Constantinople of 360. In this case the law quite explicitly grants toleration to Arians and threatens any Catholics who interfere with the right of the Arians to freedom of worship. It is probably the law of Valentinian II against which Ambrose inveighs.[2]

One may well ask how it came about that Arians were being granted toleration in the west while Theodosius' laws were harrying them in the east. Moreover we know from Ambrose that Valentinian consulted Theodosius over most major issues.[3] The situation is made even more difficult to understand by the fact that a law (XVI : 4 : 1) was issued from Constantinople to the same Prefect which is a repetition of part of this law with a few minor differences. Seeck takes it that the latter is an extract from the former put in another section by the compilers of the Code. 'CONSTANT P' then slipped in, in place of the less known 'MED'.[4] It is possible to offer another explanation, which interprets the text as

---

[1] The middle of the edict, from '*his qui sibi tantum*' to '*supplicia luituri*', is reproduced with only minor changes at XVI : 4 : 1, which was sent to the same Prefect on the same day, but from Constantinople, not Milan.

[2] Ambrose, *Sermo contra Auxent.* 16, 22, 24; *Ep.* XXI 9 ff. Cf. Rufinus XI 15 and Sozomen VII 13.

[3] Ambrose, *Ep.* XVII 12. The bishop says to the boy Emperor concerning the altar of Victory, '*Certe refer ad parentem pietatis tuae principem Theodosium, quem super omnibus fere majoribus causis consulere consuesti.*'   [4] *Regesten*, pp. 268 and 111.

it stands. XVI : 1 : 4 is addressed 'ad Eusignium', XVI : 4 : 1 is 'Eusignio'. This indicates the probability that they came into the hands of the compilers of the Code from two different collections. The one cannot be a snippet from the other. There is also some other evidence of the independent existence of XVI : 4 : 1 earlier than the compilation of the Code.[1] It is suggested therefore that the text of both laws should be accepted as it stands, that XVI : 4 : 1 is an expurgated and innocuous version of XVI : 1 : 4 and was issued by Theodosius at Constantinople.

It is possible to suggest that we have before us evidence of some liaison in religious matters between the most catholic Theodosius and Justina who had earned the title 'Jezebel', that for reasons of state the Emperor was pursuing a pro-Arian policy outside his own dominions.[2] On the other hand, the edict as it appeared at Constantinople has been carefully expurgated of anything specifically Arian. When the Arians of the east exhibited XVI : 4 : 1 as being in their favour, they were quickly repressed.[3]

Three years later when Theodosius had decided to go to war against Maximus, he issued a law commanding that the Apollinarians and other followers of various heresies were to be prohibited from all places: from the walls of the cities, from the society of honourable men, from the fellowship of the holy. They were to have no power of ordaining clergy, nor for gathering congregations either in public or private churches. They were to have no authority for making bishops; and their bishops were to be deprived of their name and lose their title. They were to betake themselves to places which might shut them off as if by a wall from human society. Also they were to be denied the right of approaching and putting appeals to the Emperor.[4]

The Apollinarians alone are named. There are distinct echoes in the law of a letter from St Gregory Nazianzen to Nectarius, and one must suppose that the saint's peculiar hate for the Apollinarians at this time explains their being singled out in the law. The law recapitulates previous measures against heretics, but adds two new details. Heretical bishops were to be deprived of their name and title and were to have no access to the Emperor.[5]

---

[1] XVI : 4 : 1 is to be found at the end of the *Dissertatio* of Maximin (Kauffmann's edition, p. 57, cf. pp. 108 f.), and it may have been put there before the Code was compiled. See also W. Bessell, *Über das Leben des Ulfilas*, Göttingen, 1860.

[2] We may compare the friendly relationship between Louis XIV and the Turks. It is perhaps worthy of note that at this time Theodosius was keen to strengthen his hold over Valentinian II in the face of Maximus' rival claim to guardianship. There is some evidence also that Theodosius was suppliant for Galla's hand in marriage.

[3] See XVI : 5 : 16.

[4] XVI : 5 : 14 of March 388. Note the interesting use of '*communio sanctorum*' and compare Kelly, *Creeds*, pp. 388 ff.

[5] Gregory, *Ep.* CCII. Cf. Ambrose, *Ep.* XIV 4 where the bishops ask that Theo-

The law *Omnes diversarum* also appeared at this time and is pretty clearly the work of Theodosius.[1] It was laid down that all who belonged to the perfidious sects and were engaged in a wretched conspiracy against God, were not to hold meetings, engage in disputations or raise altars and perform an imitation of the mysteries. The Prefect was to appoint guardians to watch the matter and hand culprits over to the judges. It is probable that in this law the Emperor is dealing with the *status quo* in Illyricum, which had been notorious for its heresies, where Justina had exercised much influence, and of which probably no part had been under Theodosius' control since 381. Such unfortunate Graeco-Roman Arians as had been spared by Gothic devastation, were in this case the object of this law. Perhaps, too, Theodosius felt he had now taken steps to clear the whole Empire of conspiracies against God, and success was bound to attend his arms. This law makes definite provision for the hunting out and trial of heretics of all kinds and therefore goes further than any previous enactment by Theodosius.

The Eunomians were the subject of a law of May 389 which with coarse vituperation called them '*spadones*'. They were to have no lawful authority to make or receive testamentary disposition, and were to have nothing in common with other men. There must have been some strong reaction, for in 394, 'on fuller consideration', the law was withdrawn.[2] Gothofredus cogently suggests that it was Tatian (to whom the law is addressed) who wished to persecute Eunomians, and Rufinus (to whom the rescinding was sent) who had it withdrawn. One can imagine that old pagan chuckling as he persecuted Christians, albeit heretical Christians. The rescinding is better explained as a means of ensuring peace while the Emperor goes to war in the west. Life (and death) must have been bewildering for the Eunomians: they lost their rights again in March 395 and regained them a few months later.[3] Gothofredus is right in drawing attention to the importance in religious legislation of the opinions and desires of the person addressed. Even a man of strong character when placed in so

dosius should cause an Apollinarian bishop to lay down his office and title after due inquiry and condemnation.

[1] XVI : 5 : 15 is headed '*idem AAA*', that is, Valentinian II, Theodosius and Arcadius, and was sent from Stobi to Trifolius the Praetorian Prefect (presumably of those parts of Italy and Illyricum which were not in Maximus' hands). Arcadius of course was not at Stobi. The law can hardly be by Valentinian. Firstly, because Italy and Illyricum were not put into Valentinian's hands after victory, it is not likely that he would be allowed to legislate for them before it. Secondly, while Justina lived she retained her Arianism and her power over her son. She did not die till the end of the year. Thirdly, it is probable that Valentinian invaded Italy by sea (Zosimus IV 45, Orosius VII 35) and was not at Stobi.

[2] XVI : 5 : 17, withdrawn by 23.   [3] XVI : 5 : 25 and 27 both by Arcadius.

isolated a position begins to depend too much on the advice of cronies and to trust them overmuch. No doubt the Emperor sitting high and lifted up, 'rubber-stamped' a good deal he had not read. But unfortunately in the case of the Eunomians, Theodosius had himself developed a special hatred.[1] It is difficult to keep personal dislike out of righteous indignation.

The last part of a law issued on the next day to the same man stated that officials who had been deprived of their office were not to enjoy the privileges which would otherwise have been theirs. It has been suggested that the Eunomians were at this time deprived of the *ius militandi*, and it is possible to cite a law of Arcadius in which he says that in accordance with the example of his father he denies heretics the right to serve.[2] No doubt the denial of this right was a logical outcome of Theodosius' legislation: we are drawing nearer to the state of affairs where civil servants must produce baptismal certificates before they can be employed, but it is not explicit in that legislation as it stands.

Theodosius' attack on the heretics reached its culminating point in June 392. He ordered that heretical clergy were to be fined ten pounds in gold and that the places where forbidden practices took place were to be confiscated if the owner had connived. If it were a tenant who was responsible, and if he were poor, he was to be beaten and deported. If rich, or if the estates were imperial or public, he was to pay the same fine.[3] The law has no high-sounding vilification of heresy but attacks more subtly. The threat to owners and stewards was probably more effective than that against clergy.[4]

During the last years of his reign Theodosius added little to his attack on the heretics. It is significant that it was at this time that his legislation against the pagans appeared, and it may be suggested that he had completed his agenda against the heretics and had turned to the next item. Before studying his relationships with paganism we must retrace our steps to the year 387 to take up the story of events where we left it.

---

[1] Socrates V 20; Sozomen VII 17; Philostorgius X 6.

[2] VIII : 4 : 16. The suggestion is made by Rauschen (p. 306). He cites XVI : 5 : 29. Cf .also XVI : 5 : 25.

[3] XVI : 5 : 21 to Tatian. Cf. also XVI : 5 : 22 of April 394 by which Theodosius directed that heretics were to have no power of either making or confirming bishops. The attack on heretical clergy seemed to appeal to the Emperor even if we are doubtful whether it had any results.

[4] The Catholics in Africa were glad of this law—Augustine, *Contra epistolam Parmeniani* I 12, 19; *Contra Cresconium* III 47, 51; *Ep.* LXXXVIII 7. The Council of Carthage of 404 asked that the law of the ten pound fine (this law) and the law of intestability (XVI : 5 : 17) be applied in certain cases to the Donatists (Mansi col. 795; Hefele-Leclerq III, pp. 155 f.).

4

Lord of the Roman World

THE RIOT AT ANTIOCH AND THE WAR AGAINST MAXIMUS

IN JANUARY 387 Arcadius held his Quinquennalia and his father his Decennalia (by anticipation).[1] The consequent demands for money from the taxpayer caused a riot at Antioch.[2] The crowd went to the baths, cut down the lamps, then pelted and pulled down the imperial statues. The military turned out and scattered the insurgents with a whiff of arrows. Those caught redhanded were immediately executed by sword, fire or wild beast and the events notified to Theodosius.[3]

The Antiochenes were in panic, for 'blasphemy' against the imperial images was a serious offence.[4] Credit must be given to Theodosius for the mildness of his first instruction. He does not seem to have flown into a rage, but to have ordered an inquiry and a most lenient preliminary punishment. A number of intercessions were made for Antioch. The best known is that of Flavian, the bishop of the city, which is recorded by St John Chrysostom.[5] The Emperor was grievously hurt by the city's insult to the dead. Flavian reminded him how when man fell and lost Paradise, God opened heaven to him. Similarly, Theodosius could now thwart the demons. He reminded him of how when Constantine was told that his image had been defaced, he passed his hand over his face and said he could find no damage. But he did not need to go so far for an example. Recently, as Easter approached, Theodosius had ordered the release of

---

[1] Rauschen p. 258; Benedictine Preface to John, 'On the Statues', *PG* 49, p. 6. On the *stasis*, see P. Petit, *Libanius et la vie municipale à Antioch*, pp. 239 ff.

[2] Libanius, *Or.* XIX 25; XXII 4. Browning in *Journal of Roman Studies*, XLII, 1952, pp. 13–20 discusses the nature of this tax.

[3] Libanius, *Or.* XXII 6–9; XIX 26 f., 32–7; *Vita* 252; John, *Hom.* V 3, *PG* 49 col. 73, XV 1 (col. 154), III 6 (col. 56).

[4] Ambrose, *Expositio in Psalmum* CXVIII Iod (X) 25. *PL* 15 col. 1340. Cf. Basil, *Comment. in Isaiam Prophetam* XIII, *PG* 30 col. 589. See also Pseudo-John Chrysostom in *PG* 56 col. 489 (he was probably Severianus of Gabala, *PW* II 2 (n.s.) 1930 ff.) and H. Kruse, *Studien zur offiziellen Geltung des Kaiserbildes*, Paderborn, 1934. Cf. also IX : 38 : 6 and IX : 44 : 1.

[5] *Hom.* XXI 2, col. 213 f.

prisoners and said he wished he could resurrect the dead. Here was that very opportunity. Flavian's appeal was successful. The Emperor pardoned the city. It remains a puzzle why the man who acted so nobly in this case, ordered a most bloody massacre a few years later when the Thessalonians killed a barbarian officer.

In the same year as the riot at Antioch, Maximus invaded Italy, and Valentinian fled to Thessalonica. The flight to Thessalonica was probably not a flight to Theodosius, for had that been the case, he would have gone to Constantinople. He was presumably continuing the struggle against the usurper from his own eastern domains. Maximus and others could well have considered that the occupation of Italy was a righteous act, in that it freed that land from the Arian taint of Justina. Maximus was himself a paragon of orthodoxy.[1] Any war by Theodosius against him could hardly be given the character of a war of religion.

Zosimus says that after Valentinian and Justina had fled to Thessalonica, Theodosius visited them there; and owing to his natural laziness, was loath to go to war till he was attracted by Galla's beauty into giving in to Justina's demands.[2] This is a pretty story, though it is probable that the marriage had already taken place, but in either case his existing or newly-contracted marriage with Galla ultimately committed Theodosius to war. Theodosius had perhaps encouraged Maximus to overcome Gratian, but now Maximus had exceeded his original ambitions and would have to be liquidated. This was convenient to Theodosius, for if he could get rid of Maximus, his own family could have Italy while Valentinian was thrust into the outer darkness of the western domains.

The question was whether all this could be done without ruining the Empire. Hardly a decade had passed since Hadrianople. This difficulty was overcome when John the Hermit assured him an easy victory.[3] The Persian border was secured by diplomacy, and the generosity shown to Antioch. The pagans were perhaps getting restive, for when Cynegius, the fanatically Christian Praetorian Prefect, died, he was replaced by a pagan. Flavius Eutolmius Tatianus had held office under Valens and may well have persecuted Athanasians when orthodoxy was Arian.[4] His son Proclus was made Prefect of Constantinople. The factiousness and bicker-

---

[1] *Collectio Avellana* XXXIX and XL. See also Rufinus XI 16 and Sozomen VII 13.
[2] Zosimus IV 43 f.
[3] Augustine, *De civitate* V 26; Rufinus XI 19; Palladius, *Hist. Laus.* 43.
[4] H. Grégoire in *Anatolian Studies presented to Sir William Ramsay.* See also Zosimus IV 45 and 52; and cf. Libanius, *Or.* XXX 53. Stein (*Zeitschrift für die Savigny-Stiftung, Röm. Abt.*, XLI, 1920, pp. 211-8 and *Geschichte*, p. 319) considers the possibility that another Prefect, who was a Christian, kept an eye on Tatian, but he can advance no convincing argument.

ing of the Christians was temporarily damped down by a prohibition on public religious discussions and disputes.[1]

So Theodosius proceeded towards Italy, confident of the outcome of the war, thanks to John the Hermit. Perhaps now and then he wondered, for Maximus was a good soldier, and he had long been preparing for war.[2] According to Orosius, Theodosius' was the smaller army.[3] After all, the war against Magnentius had taken three campaigns. There is a story that Theophilus, Bishop of Alexandria, sent Isidore to Rome with two letters, there to await the outcome of the war, and to hand the appropriate letter to whoever won, be it Maximus or Theodosius.[4] The chances were presumably even each way! It was a long march and the eastern army would be tired on arrival. In the matter of taking the passes into Italy, the defender had the advantage.

Contrary to all expectation, Theodosius obtained an easy victory. At Siscia, in Pannonia, his men, though breathless and covered in dust, urged their horses on with their spurs, swam the river, and engaged the enemy. The long-winded Pacatus finds it takes longer to describe than it took to happen, for no sooner had they engaged them than the enemy turned their backs and fled. Before long there was another engagement and another victory. This time Maximus' brother, Marcellinus, was in charge. Resistance was more stubborn, and the slaughter great, but soon Theodosius' men carried the day. Aemona had held out against Maximus and when Theodosius came up, gave him a tremendous welcome. Maximus seems to have lost his nerve. He shut himself in Aquileia where he was easily captured, brought before Theodosius, who was prevented from showing him mercy by his troops, and executed. So Maximus' imperial sovereignty was proved to be a usurpation. His head was sent on a tour of the provinces and arrived finally at Carthage.[5] Militarily, it only remained to clear up Gaul. The pagan general Arbogast, who had played a leading part in the war, was sent over the Alps. He soon killed Maximus' son Victor, and began to reorganize administration round himself.[6]

---

[1] XVI : 4 : 2. Nonetheless Arians set the archbishop's house afire at Constantinople (Ambrose, *Ep.* XL 13; Socrates V 13; Sozomen VII 14).

[2] Stevens (*Revue des Études Celtiques*, 1938, pp. 86 ff.) thinks the elder Theodosius' campaigns in Britain owed not a little of their success to Maximus. Rauschen (p. 282) cites the opinion of ancient authorities on Maximus.   [3] Orosius VII 35.

[4] Socrates VI 2; Sozomen VIII 2. Unfortunately for Theophilus, Theodosius was handed the letter congratulating his opponent!

[5] Pacatus, XXXIV ff., XLII and XLV. Cf. Ambrose, *Ep.* XL 23; Zosimus IV 46; Sozomen VII 14; Orosius VII 35; Olympiodorus, *FHG* IV, p. 61.

[6] Zosimus IV 47; *Chron. Min.* I, p. 298; Gregory of Tours, *Hist. Franc.* II 9; Aurelius Victor, *Epitome de Caes.* XLVIII 6.

Laws were passed stating that the honours given by Maximus were worthless and declaring that his legislation, where it had been contrary to law, was null and void.[1] Presumably these laws freed the Priscillianists from the disabilities laid upon them by Maximus. These Priscillianists were the followers of a bishop from Spain who had been accused of carrying asceticism to Manichaean extremes and of a number of rather fantastic practices including nudism. He had appealed against the decision of the Church to the Emperor Maximus who, despite the remonstrations of the bishops, especially St Martin of Tours, had condemned him to death. The extremity and unexpectedness of the punishment has puzzled historians. Some think Maximus was intent on seizing the goods of the rich supporters of Priscillian; there is also the suspicion that the Priscillianists were in some way connected with Theodosius. We have seen above that Theodosius assisted the Luciferians, and some relationship between these and the Priscillianists has been discovered. It has been suggested that Theodosius' family had connections with these heretics who came from the same part of Spain.[2] These ideas can be no more than speculations. But it is significant that after Theodosius' annulment of the acts of Maximus, a council deposed Priscillian's chief enemy, Ithacius of Ossonuba, and he was sent into exile. A veritable cult of the Priscillian martyrs grew up. Theodosius would probably not be ignorant of these things and perhaps he did not disapprove.

In the matter of persons, Theodosius was as humane as ever. No one lost his life by proscription. A few leaders and the Moorish guard were executed. According to Ambrose the very usurper's mother and daughter received kindness at Theodosius' hand. He rightly describes this as great piety and faith towards God. At Ambrose's request Theodosius released many enemies. He even forgave Symmachus for having produced a panegyric of the tyrant.[3]

The question remains as to what happened to Valentinian II. According to St Augustine, Theodosius gave him back his kingdom. After a close study of the evidence of the coins, the late J. W. E. Pearce was convinced Valentinian had but 'a shadow of sovereignty over a shadow of Empire'. It would appear that the coins of Italy followed the numismatic policy of Theodosius; Valentinian's writ ran only in the Gauls.[4] The Code also

[1] XV : 14 : 6, 7 and 8.
[2] A. d'Alès, *Priscillien et l'Espagne Chrétienne à la fin du IVe siècle*, Paris, 1936, pp. 133 f.; cf. p. 72. Lambert, 'Egeria, soeur de Galla', *Revue Mabillon*, 1937, pp. 1–42.
[3] Ambrose, *Ep.* XL 32. On Symmachus' panegyric see Socrates V 14, and Symmachus, *Ep.* II 31.
[4] Augustine, *De civitate* V 26. This view is supported by Zosimus IV 47 and Theodoret V 15. Pearce, p. xxii and his article 'The reign of Theodosius I' in *Proceedings*

shows that Valentinian was sent to rule in Gaul. He issued laws from Trèves in June and November 389 and seems to have remained beyond the Alps till his death in 392. Even this rule was nominal, for Theodosius' pagan general, Arbogast, held the power.

So then in late 388 we find Theodosius on Italian soil, *de facto* sole ruler of the Roman world, whereas about a decade before he had been but a landed aristocrat in Spain. Those about him, no doubt, were as staggered by his success as he was. One must avoid the cliché about absolute power corrupting absolutely, but the extent of the power and responsibility upon him must make it very difficult for a despotic ruler to keep his contact with normal values and the ordinary human standards of judgment. Herein Theodosius was no exception.

THE STAY IN ITALY UP TO THE MASSACRE AT THESSALONICA

Theodosius had not been in Italy many months before he had a clash with Ambrose. At Callinicum, a town of strategic importance on the Persian border, the Christian mob had burnt down and pillaged the synagogue at the instigation of the bishop. Theodosius had ordered the bishop to rebuild it, but the Bishop of Milan considered this a criminal order and forced the Emperor to reverse his decision.[1] He wrote to the Emperor to remind him that if the Roman army were found fighting for the Jews, Christ would not be able to give it victory, but only the catastrophies which the Jews had undergone. To show how the principle of Christ-the-Giver-of-Victory works in reverse, that is, how if he is annoyed he gives defeat, Ambrose cites the case of Maximus who was deserted by Christ because, when he heard a synagogue had been burnt at Rome, he sent an edict to Rome as a vindicator of public discipline. Ambrose emphasizes that Maximus only used words—the requital for giving actual punishment would be much worse.[2]

Ambrose plays on Theodosius' love of his children, and natural fear for their future. Even if Theodosius does not worry about the clemency of God for himself, he has those for whom he hopes more than for himself, their welfare, their safety, should appeal to him. He urges the Emperor not to fear his oath. The Emperor should not cancel the first letter, but supersede it. St Ambrose indicates that he has written to the Emperor in

of the *International Numismatic Congress*, London, 1936. See also his article in the *Numismatic Chronicle* (Vth series) XIV, 1934.

[1] Our primary sources are Ambrose, *Epp.* XL and XLI. It is usual to date these letters and the incident to late 388 when Timasius could be called *magister peditum* by Ambrose and not yet Consul.

[2] Ambrose, *Ep.* XL 20–22.

the hope that the matter can be cleared up privately, but if he receives no satisfaction as a result of his letter he will be forced to speak out in church.[1]

St Ambrose had in earlier struggles with the State tended to uphold the dual approach and even now he can say that just as on matters of money the Emperor consults the Treasury so on matters of religion he should consult the priests of the Lord.[2] There is a direct parallelism here between '*comites*' and '*sacerdotes*'. But now when there is a conflict between the Church and the State, by the sheer logic of his thinking, Ambrose has to say that the State's interests must be subordinated. We must admire the courage of the man who could tell a totalitarian ruler this to his face, but our admiration must not prevent us from seeing a foreshadowing of the day when, with tragic consequences to both, the Church was to attempt to dominate the State. Theodosius countermanded the rebuilding by the bishop as such, but Ambrose could not allow the State to rebuild, lest it be implicated in impiety, and he withstood the Emperor in church.

In a letter to his sister Ambrose tells her how he preached before the Emperor.[3] When Ambrose came down the Emperor said, 'You preached concerning us.' Then he said, 'I had decreed indeed too harshly about the reparation of the synagogue by the bishop, but that has been set right. The monks commit many crimes.'[4] Timasius, *magister equitum et peditum*, began to be rather vehement against the monks, but Ambrose refused to have any dealings with him. The bishop stood there for a while and then made it plain why he would not continue. He would not offer the Eucharist until the Emperor promised to end the whole inquiry—he was not satisfied with a nod, nor with the statement that he would amend the rescript. Not till the Emperor said explicitly '*Age fide mea*' did the bishop offer.[5]

Homes Dudden remarks that Theodosius gave in, not from weakness, nor on religious grounds, nor because he was convinced by Ambrose's

---

[1] *Ibid.*, 31, 33.

[2] *Ibid.*, 27. For a summary of Ambrose's position in the matter of Church and State, see S. L. Greenslade, *From Constantine to Theodosius*, pp. 71 ff.

[3] *Ep.* XLI. For the layout of the basilica see Dölger, *Antike u. Christentum* I, pp. 59 ff.

[4] The laconic masculinity of the statement is apparent; '*Re vera de Synagoga reparanda ab episcopo durius statueram, sed emendatum est. Monachi multa scelera faciunt.*' Cf. Jerome, *Ep.* XXXIX 5 (*PL* 22 col. 472)—the people say '*Genus detestabile monachorum*'. Theodosius ordered monks 'to frequent and inhabit desert places and vast solitudes' (XVI : 3 : 1 of 390, withdrawn by *lex* 2 of 392). The Emperor objected to the monks as troublers of the peace. He had nothing against monasticism as such. Isaac the Syrian introduced it to the capital in his reign.

[5] On the use of '*age*' see Dölger, *op. cit.*, p. 63. He compares Novatian's use of the elements as guarantors of an oath (Eusebius, *Hist. Eccl.* VI 43.18 f.) and thinks Ambrose used the whole eucharistic sacrifice as a seal of the promise.

E

artificial pleadings, but from political necessity.[1] It is true that his position in Italy was none too secure, and that Ambrose had a certain ability of stirring up the Catholic population, but Ambrose's power lay chiefly at Milan, at the most his influence did not reach much beyond Northern Italy. Theodosius had the whole power of the east and of victories behind him; he was in a very much better position than Valentinian II when faced by Ambrose's browbeating ways. Rather he gave in because he was at heart a Catholic of his day, respectful to the will of a bishop, a believer that Christ rewarded right conduct as prescribed by the bishop and avenged disobedience. If he harboured any resentment, that would have been natural enough for he had been humiliated: he could well think that he had been bullied by a bishop into a betrayal of his Christian duty to dispense justice and maintain law and order. Perhaps he dimly realized the flaw in the bishop's reasoning—that is, the utter falsity of the basic assumption that Christ did not want justice done, if the plaintiffs were Jews. No one could blame Theodosius if as a result of the Callinicum affair his attitude to the Church became less friendly, but there is little sign of this.[2] Just the same he would have been a fool if he had not contrasted in his own mind the reception he received in Rome, that stronghold of paganism, with the hectoring he had received from Ambrose in church.

On 13 June 389 Theodosius entered Rome in triumph.[3] Even an Emperor was bound to be impressed with reverence for the ancient capital and its thousand years of history and paganism. The Emperor presented his son Honorius to the Romans as their future ruler.[4] In the Senate Theodosius heard a panegyric delivered before him by one Latinus Pacatus Drepanius, a pagan orator from Gaul. Though this sort

---

[1] St Ambrose, p. 378. Palanque (Ambroise, p. 217) says much the same.

[2] Seeck (Gesch. V, pp. 224 ff., 529) thinks Theodosius did react in this way. He says the appointment of pagans to the great offices indicates it. But Tatian and Proclus were already in office and Nicomachus Flavian was not appointed till 390. There is nothing exceptionally favourable to paganism in the other appointments of this time (see Rauschen, pp. 303 ff., 337). Seeck also cites Libanius' honorary prefectship, but if he got one at all it is notoriously difficult to date. It is indeed possible that the Jewish patriarch was honoured at this time, but Theodosius was consistently friendly to the Jews. (Cf. Jerome, Ep. LVII 3; and XVI : 8 : 8 and 22.) The legislation concerning curiales, heretics and clerical privileges shows no unfriendliness to the Church.

[3] Seeck, Regesten, p. 275. Two laws by Valentinian from Trèves are dated 14 June 389 (IV : 22 : 3 and XI : 16 : 20), so though Socrates V 14 (by implication) and Sozomen VII 14 (explicitly) consider that Valentinian was at Rome, he was in the far-away north.

[4] On Rome's position see Alföldi, A Festival of Isis, p. 16; J. Geffcken, Ausgang des griechisch-römischen Heidentums, p. 101; Dölger, 'Rom in der Gedankenwelt der Byzantiner', in Zeitschr. für Kirchengesch. LVI, 1937, pp. 1–42; Stein, Gesch. I, pp. 321 ff. On the presentation of Honorius, see Pacatus XLVII and Claudian, VI cons. Honor. 54 ff.

of panegyric was by now a recognized literary form, and the diction and imagery were fairly standard, and though the empty verbiage makes it wearisome to read, Pacatus' panegyric is invaluable for giving us historical details of Theodosius' youth and person (4–10), of his campaign against Maximus (30–46), and of his visit to Rome (47), besides giving us some insight into the constitutional thinking of those days. Pacatus tells how the Empire was exhausted and submerged by barbarians till Theodosius rescued her (3). Wherever possible be brings out parallels between the career and rule of Theodosius and the old Roman usages and historical figures. The implicit deification of the Emperor is interesting. Spain has given them the God they behold (*deum dedit Hispania quem videmus*, *cap.* 4); Theodosius is a divine *numen* made visible (21). The divine *numen* is with him when he wars against Maximus (30). The Emperor should be one who is worshipped by the nations, to whom throughout the world private and public vows are rendered, from whom the sailor setting sail seeks calm weather, to whom he who sets out on a journey prays for his return, and from whom the soldier about to fight seeks favourable auspices. The Emperor cannot have been wholly displeased by such adulation bordering on blasphemy, for the orator was rewarded with the Proconsulship of Africa.

The Emperor's position at this time is well typified by a law he issued at Rome in which he regulated holidays.[1] The calends of January, the foundation days of Rome and Constantinople, the Paschal days and Sundays stand side by side. The Emperor is a worthy successor of Diocletian trying to preserve the inheritance of pagan Rome.[2] Personally he is a Christian and he legislates for the Church too.[3] Perhaps it was tragic for both religions and the Empire that he deserted this position.

[1] II : 8 : 19.

[2] It is clear that Theodosius was also courting the pagan senatorial aristocracy at this time for dynastic reasons. The effects of this can be seen in the promotion of Nicomachus Flavian to the Praetorian Prefectship and Symmachus later on to the Consulship. That the Emperor would even then not go on to anything really pagan is shown by his refusal to restore the Altar of Victory. (Ambrose, *Ep.* LVII 2 and 4.) The Pseudo-Prosper's story that Symmachus was dumped at the hundredth milestone for making the request is not worthy of credence (*PL* 51 col. 834 ff.).

[3] Probably Theodosius at this time inspected the work being done in connection with the rebuilding of San-Paolo-fuori-le-Mure. The apse mosaic commemorates his work. He had directed the Prefect of the City to see whether the site could be enlarged by diverting the road (*Collectio Avellana* III). Liturgical experts suggest that this enlargement led to the celebrant at the Eucharist finding himself between the altar and the people. Unfortunately this departure from the primitive position was copied elsewhere. To turn to another point—this building is one of the very few connected with the name of this Emperor. Theodosius has no great reputation as a generous builder of churches. Archaeology may yet prove this view mistaken: for instance, one of his buildings may have stood where the present Church of the Nations at Jerusalem cumbers the ground.

After a stay of three months at Rome Theodosius returned to Milan and it was there that news was brought to him of a riot at Thessalonica.[1]

THE MASSACRE AT THESSALONICA AND THE
REPENTANCE AT MILAN

During the latter part of 390 Theodosius, the first Emperor of the Roman world to be a Christian for the greatest part of his reign, ordered a massacre which in his century was outstanding as an atrocity. A charioteer beloved by the people of Thessalonica tried to rape a Gothic officer by the name of Butheric and was cast into prison.[2] After some time the people wanted his release so that he could take part in the forthcoming games. When their demand was not granted, they rose in revolt and killed Butheric. Theodosius ordered a massacre in which it is said thousands perished.[3]

We do not know why the Emperor acted in this way. It is true that he was a man of hasty temper, but this had not prevented calm, deliberate action when there was a riot at Antioch.[4] If he was in a rage over Thessalonica, he calmed down sufficiently to promise to pardon the city.[5] It is too easy to blame his temper or the officials about him.[6] Probably we have before us a calculated act of statecraft. The killing of a Goth by the Graeco-Roman population of Thessalonica would have to be exemplarily punished, otherwise Theodosius' delicately balanced policy of infusing the Empire with new blood while maintaining a certain *apartheid* would end in fiasco.[7] Riots were becoming too frequent and Thessalonica was on

[1] Socrates (V 18) tells how Theodosius changed the Roman practice by which if a woman were taken in adultery she was compelled to act as a prostitute while little bells were rung to advertise her shame. He also punished the bread *mancipes* for kidnapping men in a brothel-tavern to work in their bakehouses. These bazaar stories at most indicate that the Emperor gained a reputation as a reformer.

[2] On 6 August 390 Theodosius had ordered homosexual use to be punished by public burning (IX : 7 : 6, cf. 3). This was more in the Judaeo-Christian tradition than the Graeco-Roman as Lev. 18.22 and 20.13 indicate. The same law appears in the *Collatio legum mosaicarum et romanarum* (5.3) but is there dated to 14 May. Some scholars connect the Butheric affair with this law, but it is possibly mere coincidence.

[3] Sozomen VII 25; Rufinus XI 18; Theodoret V 17. (The Bodleian letter from Ascholius cannot be accepted as genuine; see Parmentier's edition, pp. 307 f.) Zosimus and Socrates are silent.

[4] *Epitome de Caesaribus* XLVIII 13. Cf. Claudian, *IV cons. Honor.* 266; Ambrose, *Ep.* LI 4.

[5] Ambrose, *Ep.* LI 3, 6; *De obitu Theodosii* 34. Cf. Paulinus 24; Augustine, *De civitate* V 26.

[6] Ambrose, *De obitu Theodosii* 34; Augustine, *De civitate* V 26. Theodoret (V 17) blames Rufinus, who was *magister officiorum*. Perhaps St Ambrose's Pyrrhic victory over Callinicum contributed something.

[7] Cf. Libanius, *Or.* XIX 22: the murder of the Gothic soldier by the people of Constantinople; Zosimus IV 40: Gerontius and the Goths at Tomi; Themistius, *Or.* XVI.

his line of communication. Having perpetrated a bloody massacre, the Emperor found himself confronted with an up-welling of horrified public opinion in which he himself no doubt shared, but, as he had remarked in one of his Easter amnesties, he was not able to bring the dead to life.

One day the Emperor received a private letter from Ambrose. The bishop reminded him how King David's sin had been forgiven by his repentance and his humbling himself and his offering of sacrifice. The Emperor who was an example of piety, who reached the peak of clemency, who did not allow individual felons to be put in danger, surely sorrowed that so many innocent people had perished. By repentance and penance he could regain the *pietas* which was his, but unless the Emperor repented, Ambrose could not offer the sacrifice in his presence.[1]

We do not know exactly what happened after Theodosius received St Ambrose's letter. Judging by what St Ambrose says in his funeral oration the Emperor took the advice in it, did penance and was received into communion.[2] The historians did not know of St Ambrose's letter to him and so had to reconstruct the means by which he was brought to repentance. It is possible to trace the process by which Paulinus' account, which appears to be based on legitimate inference and some expansion is magnified into the narrative given by Theodoret.[3] It is not surprising that historians take it that a straight line connects the penance at Milan with Canossa.[4] Whatever may actually have happened, people saw it as a signal victory of Church over State. For ourselves, in his humility and repentance we may see Theodosius' greatest achievement.

The disturbing domestic news that Arcadius had driven out his stepmother from the position in which Theodosius had left her, necessitated the Emperor's return to the east.[5] As he turned his back to the west little did Theodosius know that he would only return thither to put down a revolt and to die. As he set his face to go to Constantinople he could well

---

[1] *Ep.* LI. The letter was written with the bishop's own hand and sent privately. The church historians do not know of it. It is important to note that there is no formal threat of excommunication in this letter, but we may compare some other cases where Emperors and high officials ran the risk of excommunication. For instance, Basil (*Ep.* LXI) mentions Athanasius' intention with regard to a governor of Libya. When Valentinian I committed bigamy, no one spoke up (Socrates IV 31). Paulinus (19) says St Ambrose held Maximus guilty of Gratian's death, but the tyrant refused penance. Ambrose himself says nothing of this. In *Ep.* LVII 8 Ambrose threatened Eugenius with this penalty, but nothing came of it.

[2] *De obitu Theodosii* 34. Cf. Rufinus XI 18 and Augustine, *De civitate* V 26.

[3] Cf. H. Koch, 'Die Kirchenbusse des Kaisers Theodosius des Grossen in Geschichte und Legende', *Historisches Jahrbuch* XXVIII, 1907, pp. 257 ff.; van Ortroy, 'Les Vies grecques de S. Ambroise', in *Ambrosiana*, Milan, 1897; and in *Analecta Bollandiana* XXIII, 1904, pp. 417 ff. Palanque, *S. Ambroise*, pp. 238 ff.

[4] Lietzmann, *History of the Early Church* IV, p. 89.

[5] *Chron. Min.* II, p. 62. The Emperor left Milan in April 391.

anticipate the labours that would await him there. So far as the Christians were concerned, the main lines of the imperial policy had now been laid down by Theodosius; there was little new to be added to them for centuries. He had recently removed paganism's privileges at Rome and Alexandria, it remained to be seen whether he had really ended the uneasy truce which had existed since Julian's death. We turn now to the discussion of Theodosius' policy towards paganism.

5

Theodosius and Paganism

'INTER RELIGIONUM DIVERSITATES MEDIUS STETIT'

PASSAGES ARE not lacking in the ancient writers which seem to assert that from the beginning of his reign Theodosius combated the pagan religion. The Alexandrian Chronicle under 379 states that he destroyed the temples which Constantine had not shut.[1] The pagan Zosimus says, soon after he has described Theodosius' first entry into Constantinople, that everywhere in town and country, the temples of the gods were violated, and it was dangerous for anyone to consider there were gods, or even to look up into the heaven and worship what appeared in it.[2] But these writers are reflecting back to the beginning of the reign the conditions of its end. This would be easy enough to do. Even today as one reads Ambrose's statement in his funeral oration over Theodosius to the effect that he took away the images and cultus of the gentiles and obliterated their ceremonies, one is only too apt to reflect these conditions back to the reign as a whole.[3] Libanius' evidence alone is sufficient to refute the idea that in the first decade of his reign Theodosius was outstandingly severe in this respect. Libanius writing in the tenth year of Theodosius' reign says explicitly that apart from bloody sacrifice, his co-religionists could do as they pleased.[4] It is true that he never assumed the title Pontifex Maximus, but this was probably because many Roman and republican features were being dropped in the eastern Empire through sheer distance and passage of time. Theodosius in the early part of his reign remained on friendly terms with pagans like Themistius and Libanius, and promoted pagans like Tatian and Proclus to high office. If he had been so hostile to paganism from the beginning, the violent laws of 391 and 392 would hardly have been necessary. It is also noteworthy

---

[1] *Alexandrian Chronicle*, edited by Bauer and Strzygowski in *Denkschriften der kaiserlichen Akademie in Wien*, phil.-hist. Kl., LI, 1905.
[2] Zosimus IV 33.
[3] *De obitu Theodosii* 4.
[4] *Oratio* XXX (*Pro Templis*) 7 and 8.

that Zosimus, when he is describing the desperate state of affairs under Theodosius, says that the only recourse left to decent people was to pray for deliverance, for as yet they were allowed to go to the temples and worship according to their ancestral customs.[1]

The Emperor's year-by-year legislation to 391 shows a mild attitude towards paganism. He did his best to protect the legitimate rights of the pagans. Thus in regulating the cutting of trees in the sacred cypress grove at Antioch he says 'we have acceded both to ancient custom and to the decisions of our ancestors'.[2] He tried to preserve pagan works of art and the temple buildings.[3] As part of this policy in November 382 he sent a law to Palladius, dux Osdroenae.[4] The temple which was formerly dedicated to assembly and was now also open to the public, in which it was alleged images had been placed, images to be valued more as art than for their divinity, was to remain open perpetually. This was decreed by the authority of the Public Council. Nor did the Emperor allow any clandestine royal pronouncement to interfere in this matter. So that the temple might be seen by the assembly of the city and by crowded concourse, the dux was to preserve the observance of the vota, and by the authority of the royal pronouncement to allow the temple to remain open. It was to be be kept open in such a way that no one believed that the prohibited sacrifices were permitted by reason of that access being granted.

Gothofredus considers the coetus mentioned refers to the concilium of a province. The access to the temple which Theodosius was anxious to maintain was then connected with the Imperial Cult. The temple was at all events to be open for the vota publica in early January when the vows were taken for the safety of the Empire, and the associated convivia and ludi were held. These semi-magical rites which ensured the future of the Empire were certainly not considered an offence by the Emperor but as a necessary part of the machinery of state. As important as the safety of the Empire was the entertainment of the people. The Emperor's attitude to the artistic value of the idols is most enlightened, but unfortunately the

---

[1] Zosimus IV 29.

[2] X : 1 : 12 of 379. See also F. Cumont in Syria IX, 1928, pp. 106 f. and Downey in Trans. and Proc. of the American Philological Association LXX 1939, pp. 428 ff.

[3] Libanius, Or. XXI 15, cf. XIX 21. Themistius, Or. XVI 212 d, XIX 227 c.

[4] XVI : 10 : 8: 'Aedem olim frequentiae dedicatam coetui et iam populo quoque communem, in qua simulacra feruntur posita artis pretio quam divinitate metienda iugiter patere publici consilii auctoritate decernimus neque huic rei obreptivum officere sinimus oraculum. Ut conventu urbis et frequenti coetu videatur, experientia tua omni votorum celebritate servata auctoritate nostri ita patere templum permittat oraculi, ne illic prohibitorum usus sacrificorum huius occasione aditus permissus esse credatur.' The public council mentioned may be the Senate or the Consistory, and indicate that the Emperor is not wholeheartedly in favour of the law. Perhaps he is hiding behind the skirts of the council. Clearly a good deal of intrigue was afoot.

monks and the Christian rabble did not rise so high. The temple referred to in the law is probably the temple of the capital of the province, Edessa, which Libanius says was so useful in defence, and which was destroyed by the Christians.[1] The implication of this law is that temples were normally closed, but in cases where the idols and decorations were of artistic merit and at times like the taking of the *vota* they were to be open, so long as no sacrifices took place.[2]

A careful examination of the relevant laws reveals that Theodosius played no part in the disestablishment of paganism.[3]

Like his predecessors Theodosius was concerned to stop sacrifices performed with a view to consulting the future and to prevent black magic.[4] It is true that unscrupulous Christians could use such laws to attack their pagan enemies, alleging that innocent activities were really to do with illicit sacrifices, but the Emperor can hardly be blamed for that.

During these years pagans enjoyed the favour of the Emperor and if their ability or service justified it, they were promoted to the highest honours. Both consuls were pagans in 384 and 391. Tatian was Praetorian Prefect of the East at a vital time; Themistius and later Proclus were entrusted with the Prefectship of the City.

It now remains to compare this outline of Theodosius' policy towards paganism obtained from a study of the Code with the picture presented by Libanius in his *Oratio* XXX (*Pro Templis*). The importance of this evidence coming as it does from a contemporary who is moreover a pagan cannot be overestimated.[5]

Libanius says that Valentinian and Valens forbade sacrifices, but incense was excepted. This was confirmed by Theodosius' law,[6] so that

---

[1] *Pro Templis* 44.
[2] G. T. Stokes (*Dict. Christian Biogr.* IV, pp. 959 ff.) considers that Theodosius wanted the temples preserved to act as meeting places of his provincial councils. He refers to XII : 12 : 13.
[3] Julian restored many stolen temple estates. Valentinian took them back into the royal domains (X : 1 : 8). Gratian confiscated new estates (XVI : 10 : 20 refers to this—cf. Symmachus, *Relatio* III 8, 11–15; Ambrose, *Ep.* XVII 3–9, 16; *Ep.* XVIII 10 f., 16, 31; *Ob. Val.* 19 f.). The laws concerning Theodosius are X : 3 : 4 and XI : 20 : 6.
[4] XVI : 10 : 7 and 9, IX : 16 : 11, cf. IX : 38 : 7 and 8. See also F. Martroye, 'La Répression de la magie et la culte des gentils au IVe siècle', *Revue historique de droit* IX, 1930, pp. 669 ff.
[5] On the dating of the Oration to the summer of 388, see Appendix C. Libanius' Greek is so difficult that we owe a great debt to van Loy for his French translation in *Byzantion* VIII, 1933, pp. 19–39.
[6] *Or.* XXX 7 f.: '... ἀλλὰ τοῦτό γε καὶ ὁ σὸς ἐβεβαίωσε νόμος, ὥστε μὴ μᾶλλον ἀλγεῖν ἡμᾶς οἷς ἀφῃρέθημεν ἢ χάριν εἰδέναι τῶν συγκεχωρημένων. σὺ μὲν οὖν οὔθ' ἱερὰ κεκλεῖσθαι ⟨ ἐκέλευσας ⟩ οὔτε μηδένα προσιέναι οὔτε πῦρ οὔτε λιβανωτὸν οὔτε τὰς ἀπὸ τῶν ἄλλων θυμιαμάτων τιμὰς ἐξήλασας τῶν νεῶν οὐδὲ τῶν βωμῶν ...' The reference is probably to his pagan policy in general in such edicts as XVI : 10 : 7 of December 381 and XVI : 10 : 9 of May 385.

rather than grieve at what they have lost, Libanius and his co-believers are glad to see the favour contained in the concessions. Theodosius has not shut the temples, nor has he forbidden entrance to them, nor driven out of the shrines and altars fire, incense and reverence paid with other perfumes. Later Libanius explains the principle of the exception—in saying one thing was not to be done, the Emperor has permitted all other things.[1]

Libanius shows that the pagans realized Theodosius was not unconcerned that they were not Christians. He suggests that if Theodosius believed force would sincerely change them he would have used force long ago; but he has not used force because he knows it will be ineffectual (27). Libanius has to admit that the use of force by the monks had made many pagans nominally Christians, but he points out that forcible conversions are worthless, and remarks, quite rightly, that the use of violence is forbidden by the laws of the Christians which favour persuasion and consider constraint bad (28, 29). Libanius makes it clear that Theodosius' attitude had not been one of nonchalance; he wanted to change pagans but was not yet convinced that forceful action was the best way. What changed his mind remains to be seen.

Libanius says that sacrifices continue at Rome (33). No one had dared forbid them there, for the security of the state depended on these sacrifices. Sacrifices continue at the great and populous city of Serapis. Libanius points out that the fertility of Egypt depends on the propitiation of the Nile (35). Libanius is not able to point to any other exceptions to the rule. All he can say about Constantinople is that temples still exist there, though deprived of honours and few where they were many (5).[2] For Antioch, Libanius can only say that the temples of Fortune, Zeus, Athene and Dionysius have not been attacked (51).

So far we have dealt only with Theodosius' official policy as described by Libanius and as seen in the laws. Libanius and the church historians and Zosimus give us some valuable indications of what was going on behind this official façade. Libanius shows that rural celebrations in honour of the gods and festival days continued. It is hard to believe that sacrifice did not take place, though Libanius assures us it did not. It seems likely that these picnics, house-parties and celebrations were used by some as 'cloud-cover' for sacrifice. However this may be, Libanius gains

---

[1] *Or.* XXX 18: '. . . ἀλλ' ἐν εἰπὼν δεῖν μὴ ποιεῖν τἄλλα πάντα ἀφῆκας.'

[2] It is possible to fill out this description a little from Malalas, who says that Constantine had dismantled the temples there (Bonn ed. p. 345), and Theodosius turned a temple of Aphrodite into a coach-house for the Praetorian Prefect (*ibid.*, p. 324).

his point that libations and celebrations, carried out by pagans without sacrifice were not expressly forbidden by law (17 ff.).

Just as the pagans were able to use the existing laws to carry on their practices, certain Christians were using the law as an excuse to transgress its spirit. It is possible to reconstruct from Libanius what the monks were doing. If they heard that a district had something which it was possible to plunder, straightway they alleged that sacrifices and dreadful rites took place there; and expedition must be made against it: then the security forces came up, for this was the name these robbers gave themselves.[1] Most of the activity described by Libanius seems to have been carried out irrespective of the law, and the will of the Emperor. He says these men clad in black who eat more than elephants, though the law is still in force, rush against the temples with wood and stones and iron, those that are without these, with hands and feet. Roofs are destroyed, walls undermined, images thrown down, altars smashed; the priests have to be silent or die. When the first temple is down, they run to the second and third, and, against the law, join trophy to trophy. They dare this in the towns, and even more in the country. They go through the land like torrents, ravaging the countryside through destroying the temples, for the district where they have cut down the temple is one which has been blinded, put down, killed. The temples are the soul of the country. They say they war against the temples, but this is a pretext for looting. Not content with the contents, they say the land itself is sacred, and many have thus been deprived of their patrimony. The unfortunates who had lost their goods, went to a Shepherd, for thus they termed a man not at all good, and told him what they had suffered; this Shepherd approved the action of the marauders, and drove off the sufferers saying that they should count it an advantage that they had not undergone worse (8, 9, 11).

It would seem that the sufferers could not appeal to anyone other than the local bishop, for 'the Shepherd' here most probably refers to the bishop. The local governors were either all pro-Christian, which seems unlikely, or they were so overawed by powerful persons, that they were powerless to act. One may ask who were these persons. Libanius twice in this Oration mentions the Consistory, and each time he seems to consider it hostile.[2] Also among the arguments which Libanius mentions the Christians brought forward in self-defence, he says they asserted that it was good for the world and humanity to bring the temples to nothing,

---

[1] *Or.* XXX 12: 'κἂν ἀκούσωσιν ἀγρὸν ἔχειν τι τῶν ἁρπασθῆναι δυναμένων, εὐθὺς οὗτος ἐν θυσίαις τέ ἐστι καὶ δεινὰ ποιεῖ καὶ δεῖ στρατείας ἐπ' αὐτὸν καὶ πάρεισιν οἱ σωφρονισταί, τοῦτο γὰρ ὄνομα τίθενται ταῖς λῃστείαις, εἰ μὴ καὶ μικρὸν εἶπον.'
[2] *Ibid.*, 3 and 48.

that they have done it on the Emperor's behalf and have done well by his house.[1] Now Libanius would not bring forward these arguments which are highly damaging to his side, if he had not some reason to expect that they were well-known; he has brought them forward to refute them, and this he does with some care. It seems at least possible to suggest that Theodosius' attitude to paganism had given the impression that the destruction of paganism was not unwelcome and the effects of it not unbeneficial to his interests.

The most important person who was favouring the destruction of the temples is not by name mentioned by Libanius. He says that if one examined the matter accurately, it had nothing to do with Theodosius, but it is the work of the foul fellow who has deceived him (46). This man was probably Cynegius, the crony and countryman of the Emperor who used his position as Praetorian Prefect of the East from 384 to 388 to attack paganism.[2] It was probably he who gave his backing to the commando raids carried out by the monks. He may well be the general to whom Libanius refers when he says that it is shameful to see an army warring against the temples, the property of the Emperors, and the general set over them exhorting them against the ancient buildings.[3] Thus it is likely that Cynegius was behind the destruction of the temple on the Persian frontier, probably at Edessa, described by Libanius.[4] He says that this colossal temple, so useful for defence and observation of enemy territory, so full of works of art, is no more. He then goes on to accuse not Theodosius, but the man who has deceived him. Cynegius may also have had a hand in the destruction of the temple of Aegae.[5]

It was Cynegius who was ultimately responsible for the destruction of the great temple of Zeus at Apamea. Theodoret says that when Marcellus was bishop there arrived at Apamea the Governor ($\H{v}\pi\alpha\rho\chi o\varsigma$) of the East bringing with him two chiliarchs and their followers. Because of the soldiers, the people were silent. They tried to destroy the temple of Zeus, but the building was too strong. Marcellus took to prayer; then by the device of undermining the columns of the temple, and propping it with wood, which was then set afire, and after a struggle with a demon, the

---

[1] *Ibid.*, 30 and 49.

[2] Seeck, *Gesch.*, p. 527 and *PW* XI 2527 f.; van Loy, *Byzantion* VIII, 1933, p. 403.

[3] Libanius, *Or.* XXX 43. The whole passage is noteworthy for the brilliance of the way in which Libanius manages to point out politely that the Emperor, in letting the temples be destroyed, is as sane as the man who dumps his own purse in the sea or a captain who commands a sailor to throw away the oar.

[4] *Ibid.* 44 ff.

[5] Petit, *Byzantion* XXI, 1951, p. 301, basing his argument on Heikel's edition of Eusebius, *Vita Constantini*, p. 103, lines 21 ff., which is said to be a later interpolation.

temple was destroyed.[1] It is noticeable that the actions of Marcellus (who it seems destroyed other temples too) had official backing: Theodoret says he was the first to use the law as a weapon. The troops were not monastic rabble, but soldiery. On the other hand, the people did not support the action; they had to be terrorized into silence.[2]

It is the measure of Theodosius' greatness, laziness or duplicity that he was able to continue such a policy which held together two mutually contradictory ideas. For the moment, having allowed his policy to become too heavily weighted to one side by the anti-pagan Cynegius, it is significant that in 388 he appointed a pagan, Tatian, to be Praetorian Prefect of the East. We have seen in the two preceding chapters how Theodosius continued his kindly policy towards paganism after his defeat of Maximus. We may conclude this discussion of Theodosius' policy towards paganism from 379 to 391 by saying that while Theodosius sat in divine state surrounded by his court, maintaining an official policy of toleration reminiscent of that of Valentinian I in that it only forbade divination and sacrifice, powerful subordinates, and crowds of monks, were actively fighting paganism, and destroying temples. It is not possible to say which of the two attitudes was Theodosius' own; perhaps we should say both were his own. They were ultimately incompatible, but while he could maintain both, the desires of the Christians were being met, and the pagans had reason to remain at peace, for though they wept because of their deprivations, they were glad that so much was left them.[3]

THE ANTI-PAGAN LAWS OF 391 AND THE DESTRUCTION
OF THE SERAPEUM

We are now in a position to discuss the great anti-pagan laws of 391. In February the Emperor ordered that no one was to pollute himself with sacrifices nor kill an innocent victim nor approach the shrines, nor hallow the temples and reverence images formed by human handiwork, lest he became guilty before divine and human sanctions. The judges were to be bound by this principle, that if any *inlustris* or *spectabilis*[4] follower of profane rites entered any temple, either on the road or in the city, for

---

[1] Theodoret V 21. The Governor was Deinias, who was subordinate to Cynegius. See Petit, p. 301 and G. Downey, *A study of the Comites Orientis and the Consulares Syriae*, Princeton, 1939, p. 13; but cf. Valesius at *PG* 82 col. 1590.

[2] Cf. Libanius, *Ep* 1053—the town of Apamea was faithful to its gods, though their worship was forbidden.

[3] Libanius, *Or.* XXX 7.

[4] This adopts Seeck's conjectural insertion of '*si quis inlustris vel spectabilis*' before '*profano ritui*' (cited by Mommsen in his critical apparatus to this law).

purposes of adoration, he should be compelled to pay fifteen pounds of gold forthwith, and his department should pay an equal sum with the same speed, unless they had resisted the judge and reported the matter immediately with public attestation. Consulars should pay six, and their departments a similar sum, *correctores* and *praesides* should pay four and their staff a similar sum equally allotted.[1]

The minimizing view of this law is that in only applying at Rome what had long been the rule in the eastern Empire, it takes up the legislation of Valentinian and Valens which prohibited all bloody sacrifice lest it should be used as cover for divination and the black arts. Moreover the second part of the law fining persons who go into the temples to worship is only concerned with people of high rank and official position. Yet it is clear that the object of the law is to prohibit not just the kind of sacrifice which it is feared may be turned into divination, but official public sacrifice at Rome. With sacrifice goes the worship of images in temples. Pagan public sacrificial worship was now to end at Rome, where such worship had gone on for more than a thousand years. The Emperor's words indicate that he was now sure that divine sanctions were against the continuance of the old cultus; presumably he no longer feared that the cessation of sacrifice would mean the end of the Empire. As *Cunctos populos* (XVI : 1 : 2) of 380 had been a call to the heretics to prepare for battle, so *Nemo se hostiis polluat* was a trumpet blast to the pagans, which as we shall see they heard and understood. It is not likely that Theodosius underestimated the resolution of the pagans at Rome and their power to upset all his dynastic plans in the west; his assurance that this was the will of God made him reckless of all else.

In a law of 16 June 391 the Emperor applied the measures of *Nemo se hostiis polluat* to Alexandria, the other great pagan city which had e..; ved exceptional privileges in the matter of pagan cultus.[2] The power of sa ·i-ficing was to be accorded to none, no one was to go round temples (.

---

[1] XVI : 10 : 10 sent on 24 February 391 from Milan to Albinus. The received te. names him as Praetorian Prefect, but he was Prefect of Rome (Tillemont, *Histoirε* 44th note on Theodosius, cf. Rauschen, p. 338). '*Nemo se hostiis polluat, nemo insontem victimam caedat, nemo delubra adeat, templa perlustret et mortali opere formata simulacra suspiciat, ne divinis adque humanis sanctionibus reus fiat. Iudices quoque haec forma contineat, ut, si quis profano ritu deditus templum uspiam vel in itinere vel in urbe adoraturus intraverit, quindecim pondo auri ipse protinus inferre cogatur nec non officium eius parem summam simili maturitate dissolvat, si non et obstiterit iudici et confestim publica adtestatione rettulerit. Consulares senas, officia eorum simili modo, correctores et praesides quaternas, apparitiones illorum similem normam aequali sorte dissolvant.*'

[2] XVI : 10 : 11 from Aquileia. It has an uncommon dual address—to Evagrius the Augustal Prefect and Romanus, Count of Egypt. '*Nulli sacrificandi tribuatur potestas, nemo templa circumeat, nemo delubra suspiciat. Interclusos sibi nostrae legis obstaculo profanos aditus recognoscant adeo, ut, si qui vel de diis aliquid contra vetitum sacrisque*

procession?), no one was to reverence shrines. Men were to know that the law prohibited them from access to the temples for purposes of worship. Offenders would receive no mercy. Judges who violated this law during their time of office were to be fined fifteen pounds in gold, and their office staff a similar sum unless they had opposed the judge with united force.

The fourth-century Emperors since Diocletian had loved regulation and uniformity and the rule against public sacrifice had been laid down before Theodosius' day by Valentinian and Valens. The rule would inevitably be applied to Rome and Alexandria when a Christian Emperor arose who felt himself in a position strong enough to attack in safety these strongholds of paganism, and who had sufficient trust in the God of the Christians to believe that the safety of the Empire did not depend on the demons of Rome, and the fertility of the Nile was not conditional upon the correct propitiation of the gods. He had also of course to believe whole-heartedly that the God of the Christians was offended by pagan ceremonies.

The sending of this law is sometimes connected with the destruction of the Serapeum. If this is so, it has to be pointed out that the law nowhere provides for any measures which would in themselves have led on to that destruction. The temple of Serapis at Alexandria was to the pagans, after the great temples of Rome, the most outstanding of their shrines. The great temple was razed to the ground by the Christians probably in 391.[1] The prime mover in the destruction was the stormy petrel Theophilus, Bishop of Alexandria, and it is exceedingly difficult to see exactly what part was played in the affair by Theodosius. Our primary source is the pagan Eunapius, whose account is given in the form of a digression, as proof that there was something more than human in the philosopher Antoninus.[2] When he died the worship of the gods at Alexandria and at the Serapeum came to an end and even the buildings were destroyed. The temple at Canopus was also destroyed. He mentions Theodosius as the reigning monarch, but nowhere implicates him in what was done. He definitely implicates Theophilus, the Pope of Alexandria, and the Prefect

---

molietur, nullis exuendum se indulgentiis recognoscat. Iudex quoque si quis tempore adminis-
trationis suae fretus privilegio potestatis polluta loca sacrilegus temerator intraverit,
quindecim auri pondo, officium vero eius, nisi conlatis viribus obviarit, parem summam
aerario nostro inferre cogatur.'

[1] Ammianus Marcellinus xxii.16.12. Libanius, *Or.* XXX 35. On the dating see Appendix C.

[2] Eunapius, *Vitae philosophorum et sophistarum*, Antoninus (Boissonade, p. 43 f., Didot, p. 471 f.). A. D. Nock ('Two Notes', *Vigiliae Christianae* III, 1949, p. 56) points out that St Augustine (*De divinatione daemonum*) knew of this prophecy.

and the commander of troops; for, having named them, he continues to say that these were the men who raided the temples and destroyed the Serapeum. Eunapius emphasizes the element of greed amongst the motives of the Christians—he says that they would have taken away the floor too, but the flagstones were too heavy to remove. He goes on to speak of monks being brought in; they were presumably the shock-troops in these lightning offensives by Christian marauders.

Rufinus, who is here one of our earliest Christian sources, states that Constantius was said to have given to the Arians a certain public building which was old and rather neglected. Theophilus asked this of Theodosius as he needed the space. On his entry he revealed to public derision certain pagan cult-objects which he found there. This led to a riot in which the pagans appear to have gained the upper hand, and to have carried out atrocities on captured Christians. They were under the leadership of one Olympius.[1] 'Events were reported to the Emperor. He who, in accordance with the innate mercifulness of his character, preferred to correct rather than to destroy those who went astray, wrote back that vengeance was not to be demanded for those whose blood, shed before the altars, had made them into martyrs. The glory of their sacrifice had surpassed the tragedy of their death. But for the rest, the cause of evil, the roots of discord, which came for the defence of images, ought to be completely cut away. When these were destroyed, the cause of war also would likewise be abated. And when these writings had arrived and each people (that is pagans and Christians), after a short period of truce, had come together to the temple to listen, as soon as the first page of the epistle was made known, in the beginning of which the vain superstitions of the gentiles were criticized, a mighty shout was raised by our people and amazement and fear assailed the people of the gentiles. They tried to find hiding places or began to mingle quietly with us.' Rufinus then turns aside to describe the site and building of the Serapeum, and goes on to say that when the rescript had been read, certain of the Christians were ready for the throwing down of the author of error, but some were afraid that if human hand touched the idol, the earth would dissolve in chaos, and the heaven fall. Nonetheless a Christian soldier struck, and the idol was broken up.[2]

Later, after he has described how the Nile measure was taken from the

---

[1] On him see also 'Suidas' *s.v.* 'Olympos' (*sic*). The article 'Sarapis' also assists our understanding of the destruction. Possibly both are based on Eunapius.

[2] Rufinus XI 22 f.: '. . . *res gesta ad imperatorem refertur. ille qui ingenita mentis clementia errantes mallet emendare quam perdere, rescribit illorum quidem vindictam, quos ante aras sanguis fusus martyres fecit, non esse poscendam, in quibus dolorem interitus*

Serapeum and placed in a church, Rufinus adds that when this was told to the Emperor, he is said to have stretched his palms to the sky and said with the utmost joy, 'Thanks be to thee, O Christ, because blindness of so long standing has been done away without the ruin of that mighty city.'[1] Rufinus, a man credulous enough, has to introduce this last story as hearsay. It seems clear that the Emperor did not explicitly order the destruction, though it has to be admitted that Rufinus' words can all too easily be misunderstood to state this and the Christian mob could take a hint—a wink is as good as a nod. If Rufinus has correctly reported the Emperor's letter, Theodosius' ambiguity at a vital place was either cowardly or criminal.

It seems clear then that Theodosius did not explicitly order the destruction of the Serapeum. This destruction is another example of the disconnection between the Emperor's legal and official policy and the effects of the advantage unruly subordinates took of his attitude and his likely reaction if confronted with a *fait accompli*. On the other hand, even if Theodosius did not order the destruction of the Serapeum he was an accomplice after the event, and it can be safely asserted that the destruction would not have taken place with the co-operation of the governor and troops unless it was known that the Emperor was likely to approve of such actions. These actions were in flagrant violation of the law, for nowhere in the laws known to us from reliable sources does Theodosius order the general destruction of temples. His official policy had been to shut the temples and to preserve the buildings, especially if they contained works of art. The Serapeum was such a building, in itself a monument of the great culture for which Theodosius professed to care.

The destruction of the Serapeum dealt a blow to the position of the Roman Emperors in Egypt. They had taken over from the Ptolemies the old priestly position of the Pharaohs, and had gained pagan support thereby. With the weakening of the pagan party in Egypt, and the definite dissociation of the Emperor from paganism, this support for the

---

superaverit gloria meritorum; de cetero vero malorum causam radicesque discordiae, quae pro simulacrorum defensione veniebant, penitus debere succidi, quibus exterminatis etiam bellorum causa pariter conquiesceret. cumque haec scripta venissent et velut post indutias parvi temporis ad audiendum uterque populus convenissent ad templum statim ut prima epistulae pagina reserata est, in cuius exordio vana gentilium superstitio culpabatur, clamor a nostris immensus adtollitur, stupor ac pavor gentilium populos invadit, latebras unusquisque quaerere, angustos fugae calles rimari aut nostris se latenter immergere. . . .' Cf. Sozomen VII 20. It would be of great interest if one could trace the course of this story to its modern descendant in Pakistan in the legends of Mahmud of Ghazni, the Idolbreaker.

[1] Rufinus XI 30. Socrates (V 16), Sozomen (VII 15) and Theodoret (V 22) have some independent material, but as is so often the case in this synoptic problem, Rufinus (or the source which he is closely following) is primary.

F

Emperors also grew weaker, and in due course the Bishops of Alexandria took over the Pharaonic position. The Popes of Alexandria had one force less to curb their pride.

The events at Alexandria must have led to unrest and uneasiness throughout the Empire. Other temples in the east seem to have been attacked at about this time. Sozomen, after his account of the destruction of the Serapeum goes on to say that there existed yet in certain cities pagans who fought eagerly on behalf of the temples, in Arabia at Petraea and Areopolis, in Palestine at Raphia and Gaza, in Phoenicia at Heliopolis, in Syria at Apamea by the river Axius.[1] There is no reason however to suppose that there was a wholesale and widespread attack upon temples and images throughout the Empire, for we hear of no more such destruction under Theodosius, but now and then learn of destruction going on during the next reigns.

Theodosius had been the means by which a severe blow at official and public paganism had been struck, but it was dying already of decrepitude and it is a pity to risk being accused of murdering a person whom the course of nature will remove before long. It is not possible to watch without pity the death-throes of a religion which had not been devoid of a certain nobility of its own. In the east it remained to eliminate the pagan high officials Theodosius had himself put in. In the west paganism refused to die so easily and a war had to be fought to administer the *coup de grâce*.

PAGANISM ATTACKED AND RESURGENT

Some time after the Emperor's return to Constantinople in July 391, a struggle for power broke out at court. Using the basest of methods, Rufinus, a catholic from Aquitaine, ousted the pagan Tatian and his son Proclus.[2] Happily it is not necessary to go far into the course of this melancholy affair. There may however be a connection between the fall of the pagan Praetorian Prefect and the decision of the pagan Arbogast in the far west to rid himself of Theodosius' suzerainty, but it is impossible to decide its exact nature. Valentinian II died on 15 May 392, and Eugenius, Arbogast's protégé, was not elevated till 22 August.[3] Therefore

---

[1] Sozomen VII 15. We may also compare the exploits of Martin in the west.

[2] Zosimus IV 51 f. This account is borne out by earlier sources and is therefore dependable: Eunapius, fragment 59 in *FHG* IV, p. 40; Claudian, *In Ruf.* I 234 ff.; Asterius, *Hom. in fest. Kal.*, *PG* 40 col. 224 f. Rufinus' piety is attested by his building of a church to St Peter and St Paul and installing there a society of monks. He was baptized amidst great pomp during the dedication of the church (Sozomen VIII 17, Hefele-Leclerq II 1, pp. 97 ff.).

[3] Epiphanius, *De mensuris et ponderibus* 20; *Chron. Min.* I, pp. 298, 517. Tatian's fall was probably in the summer of 392 (Palanque, *Essai*, pp. 63 ff.).

the interaction could have been either way, but on the whole it looks as if Tatian's fall decided Arbogast that reconciliation was no longer possible, so he ceased to wait for Theodosius to act and elevated Eugenius.

We left Valentinian II after the defeat of Maximus nominally ruling the territories beyond the Alps with Arbogast wielding the reality of power. Nobody could tell what were Theodosius' plans—possibly he had none beyond the vague intention of giving Honorius Italy. The arrangement creaked along well enough till Valentinian became restive.[1] The Senate, or part of it, made another request for the return of the *ara* and though the Consistory was in favour of granting it, Valentinian refused.[2] This restiveness may have alarmed Arbogast and as a pagan he would not like the rejection of the Senate's request.[3] Perhaps he decided to make away with Valentinian. On 15 May 392 Valentinian was found dead in mysterious circumstances.[4] For some months Arbogast ruled in the name of Theodosius and his son.[5] Theodosius did nothing. At Milan the crying of the dead man's sisters and the body of Valentinian in the summer heat embarrassed Ambrose.[6] Arbogast had time to think things over. On 22 August he elevated to the purple one Eugenius.

This Eugenius was of Roman stock; he had taught rhetoric, and then became one of the *magistri scriniorum*. His patron Richomer had commended him to Arbogast and thus he came to be at court in Gaul. He was a Christian. Ambrose in writing to him can speak of 'the God of our fathers' and ask him why he offers his gifts to Christ. Paulinus and Sozomen call him a Christian.[7] It is true that an examination of his coins reveals no distinctively Christian emblem or motif but this means nothing, for Theodosius himself did not shine in this respect.[8] Eugenius' Julianic beard makes no apostate of him. He could consult a pagan oracle, but

[1] Zosimus (IV 53) tells a story of Valentinian trying unsuccessfully to dismiss Arbogast. Philostorgius (XI 1) says he tried to kill Arbogast with a sword. In John of Antioch (frag. 187, *FGH* IV, p. 608) we are told that Arbogast killed one of Valentinian's friends when the friend was sheltering under the Emperor's robe. Cf. 'Suidas' *s.v.* 'Abrogastes' (*sic*).
[2] Ambrose, *Ep.* LVII 5; *De ob. Val.* 19, 20, 52, 55, 56.
[3] That he was a pagan is clear from Paulinus 26 and 31, and Ambrose, *In Psalm.* XXXVI 25. 'Suidas' who is here probably using Eunapius (frag. 53), is full of his praise. Cf. Zosimus IV 53. Praise by Eunapius and Zosimus is often an indication that its object is a pagan.
[4] Rauschen, pp. 361 f., collects all the evidence.
[5] He struck many coins in Arcadius' name, Pearce, pp. xxiv f. See also his article 'Eugenius and his eastern colleagues' in *Numismatic Chronicle*, 5th series, XVII, 1937, pp. 1–27.
[6] *Ep.* LIII 5.
[7] Ambrose, *Ep.* LVII 8 ff.; Paulinus 26; Sozomen VII 22.
[8] Cohen VIII p. 173 no. 3 records a *chi rho* on one of his coins but Pearce has no trace of it.

Christian political leaders do that today without prejudicing their faith in their own eyes. Philostorgius says roundly that he was a Greek by religion, but his evidence cannot stand by itself.[1] Probably Eugenius was a typical product of second generation educated class Christianity.

At first Arbogast and Eugenius may have hoped to enjoy the recognition granted to Maximus while he had remained beyond the Alps. They sent an embassy to Theodosius and it was received with an evasive but not unfriendly answer.[2] As time wore on, Eugenius seems to have allowed himself to enter into an alliance with the pagan aristocracy of Rome. Eugenius and his master do not seem at the beginning to have been eager to ally with the pagans. Two deputations sent by the Senate met with no success, only the third was rewarded.[3] We may presume that if Theodosius had been willing to compromise, the Arbogast regime would not necessarily have become pagan in tone, but that when they were certain of Theodosius' opposition they had to find all the allies they could muster and so gave in to the third deputation. Even then the alliance with paganism was not overt. The pagan lands were granted to pagan individuals, not to the temples as such. Though later on Theodosius' war with Eugenius was alleged to be a holy war to defend the existence of Christianity, Theodosius' opposition to Eugenius at this point could not have been religious, for Eugenius had not yet come down on the pagan side, nor, so far as we know, given any sign of a pronouncedly pro-pagan policy.

Late in 392 Theodosius at last openly attacked paganism as such by legal action.[4] He ordered that no one was to slay innocent victims to

---

[1] Philostorgius XI 2.

[2] Zosimus IV 54; Rufinus XI 31; John of Antioch frag. 187.

[3] Ambrose, *Ep.* LVII 6; Palanque, *Ambroise*, p. 547 dates this letter to autumn 393. Rauschen's dating to spring 393 seems more acceptable.

[4] XVI : 10 : 12 to Rufinus, Praetorian Prefect of the East: '*Nullus omnino ex quolibet genere ordine hominum dignitatum vel in potestate positus vel honore perfunctus, sive potens sorte nascendi seu humilis genere condicione fortuna in nullo penitus loco, in nulla urbe sensu carentibus simulacris vel insontem victimam caedat vel secretiore piaculo larem igne, mero genium, penates odore veneratus accendat lumina, inponat tura, serta suspendat. Quod si quispiam immolare hostiam sacrificaturus audebit aut spirantia exta consulere, ad exemplum maiestatis reus licita cunctis accusatione delatus excipiat sententiam conpetentem, etiamsi nihil contra salutem principum aut de salute quaesierit. Sufficit enim ad criminis molem naturae ipsius leges velle rescindere, inlicita perscrutari, occulta recludere, interdicta temptare, finem quaerere salutis alienae, spem alieni interitus polliceri. Si quis vero mortali opere facta et aevum passura simulacra inposito ture venerabitur ac ridiculo exemplo, metuens subito quae ipse simulaverit, vel redimita vittis arbore vel erecta effossis ara cespitibus, vanas imagines, humiliore licet muneris praemio, tamen plena religionis iniuria honorare temptaverit, is utpote violatae religionis reus ea domo seu possessione multabitur, in qua eum gentilicia constiterit superstitione famulatum. Namque omnia loca, quae turis constiterit vapore fumasse, si tamen ea in iure fuisse turificantium probabuntur, fisco nostro adsocianda censemus. Sin vero in templis fanisve publicis aut in aedibus agrisve alienis tale quispiam sacrificandi genus exercere*

images which lacked sense. Nor was anyone to venerate *lares*, *genii* or *penates*. Immolation for either sacrifice or reading of entrails was forbidden. Informers were to be encouraged. He poured scorn on people who venerated images made by human hands and reverenced things they themselves had made. Such people caused injury to religion and violated the holy. Houses and places where pagan rites had gone on were to be confiscated. A fine of twenty-five pounds in gold was imposed on anyone who sacrificed or who connived. The law concluded with threats against officials who took no action against offenders.

Public sacrificial worship in temples and shrines except at Rome and Alexandria had been at least legally brought to an end before Theodosius' time. He had himself eliminated the exceptions. Now Theodosius forbids every kind of pagan religious practice—bloody sacrifice, incense, family devotion to *lares* and *penates* in the home, as well as rustic rites. The penalties are not as heavy as they might be, for nowhere in this law is death imposed. Also there is no good evidence that the law was applied in the west, yet its contents would become known in official circles there. Its effects in turning powerful pagan groups against Theodosius must have been immediate; it may well have indicated to Eugenius that he would find allies amongst the pagans and so have aided his decision to enter Italy.

The remarks about idols lacking sense and the stupidity of the heathen's behaviour are commonplaces of Jewish and Christian iconoclastic polemic, which began before Isaiah and came down to the Christian fathers.[1] It is a little surprising to find a Roman Emperor echoing such futile derision, for even the lowest and rudest of their devotees must have known he was reverencing not the idols but what they stood for. It would have little effect on the educated pagan (and only the educated were likely to read the law) other than needlessly annoying him. Probably the law was drawn up by some ecclesiastical lawyer, and it served to please and encourage fatuous Christians who desired to think their opponents were fools. That it was addressed to Rufinus may explain some of the language.

The scope of this law is so wide that it would be almost impossible to

temptaverit, si ignorante domino usurpata constiterit, viginti quinque libras auri multae nomine cogetur inferre, coniventem vero huic sceleri par ac sacrificantem poena retinebit. Quod quidem ita per iudices ac defensores et curiales singularum urbium volumus custodiri, ut ilico per hos comperta in iudicium deferantur, per illos delata plectantur. Si quid autem ii tegendum gratia aut incuria praetermittendum esse crediderint, commotioni iudiciariae subiacebunt; illi vero moniti si vindictam dissimulatione distulerint, triginta librarum auri dispendio multabuntur, officiis quoque eorum damno parili subiugandis.'

[1] Cf. Isa. 44.9–20. Gothofredus gives a list which includes Tertullian, Minucius Felix, Origen, Lactantius, Arnobius, Prudentius and Augustine. He also compares Horace, *Sermonum* I.viii.1–3.

apply it in every detail. Such application as it could receive would depend on the local governors, and inevitably would vary from place to place. Theodosius himself feared that his officials would not enforce it, and had to threaten them. Arcadius and Honorius in repeating his legislation had to remind governors of their duty and they state that these men had condoned offences against previous edicts.[1] One cannot imagine how domestic worship of *lares* and *penates* could be stopped by an imperial command, unless everybody's home was to become the prey of the informer and official investigator.

Theodosius obviously considered it was time to permit a climax to be reached. In the east he was given a certain passive receptivity, but in the west he was met with violent reaction. The pagans in the west rallied and they found powerful friends ready to hand who had also been driven to arms by Theodosius' apparently double-dealing ways.[2]

Eugenius decided there was nothing to be gained by keeping out of Italy, so in 393 he crossed the Alps. He allied himself firmly to the pagans by allowing the restoration of the altar of Victory in the Senate House, by giving back pagan estates and by accepting Nicomachus Flavian, the leader of the pagans, as his Praetorian Prefect.[3] War was now inevitable. The cynical historian may well consider it a sordid struggle between an ambitious upstart and a scheming dynast into which religion was dragged sideways. Indeed, no man's springs of action are pure, no one fails to deceive himself about his own motives. Few powerful men can resist using anything that lies to hand, including religion, to perpetuate their own control of things, even if it be through their children. Yet it would be an injustice to Theodosius to imply that he was just a dynast at this point. For him, as for his contemporaries, it was a battle *à l'outrance* between Christianity and paganism.

---

[1] XVI : 10 : 13. Cf. Augustine, *Ep.* XCI and XCVII.

[2] The pagan resurgence of 393/394 has a full and sufficient literature. See especially G. Boissier, *La Fin du paganisme*, 2 vols, Paris 1891; F. Cumont, *Les Religions orientales dans le paganisme romain*, 4e ed., Paris 1929; J. Geffcken, *Der Ausgang des griechisch-römischen Heidentums*; A. D. Nock's edition of Sallustius, *Concerning the Gods*, Cambridge, 1926 and O. Seeck's edition of Symmachus, *Mon. Ger. Hist., auct. ant.*, VI 1, Berlin, 1883. The writer read a paper on the subject at the International Patristic Conference of 1959.

[3] See Homes Dudden, *St Ambrose*, p. 424, Piganiol, *L'Empire chrétien*, p. 264 and Palanque, *Ambroise*, p. 279. Nicomachus may already have been in this post as Theodosius' nominee, though it is just possible that he had been dismissed in favour of Apodemius who appears as *p(raef.) pr(aet.) Illyrici et Afric.* (but not *Italiae* as Seeck, *Regesten*, p. 279 states) on 15 February 392. Africa remained with Theodosius (see IX : 7 : 9). Theodosius probably found Gildo's support worth the ignoring of Gildo's Donatist friend, Optatus of Timgad.

6

Victory and Death

THE BATTLE OF THE FRIGIDUS

SO AT last it was open war between Christianity and paganism. As they left Milan the leaders of the pagan army boasted that on their victorious return they would turn Ambrose's basilica into a stable and force the clergy to serve.[1] Statues of the Thunderer were set up by the battle-field. Hercules appeared on the banners.[2] Nicomachus Flavian consulted the entrails and was assured of success.[3] The fulfilment of a prophecy which promised the end of Christianity was confidently anticipated.[4] On his side Theodosius too prepared as for a holy war. He consulted John the Hermit and was promised victory after great slaughter. His spiritual re-armament continued with fastings, prayers and processions.[5] Nor did he neglect the more material aspects of success in warfare. Though the Christian historians would have us believe his was the smaller army, he had certainly collected a vast army of Goths, 'Romans' and orientals. He left his two sons at Constantinople and departed for the west in May 394. He drew close to the enemy early in September.[6]

[1] Paulinus 31.

[2] Augustine, *De civitate* V 26; Theodoret V 24.

[3] Rufinus XI 33.

[4] Augustine *De civitate* XVIII 53. Christianity was to come to an end after 365 years; 29 + 365 = 394, the year of Flavian's consulship. Cf. Rufinus XI 33.

[5] Rufinus XI 32 f., cf. 19; Sozomen VII 22, 24, 29; Theodoret V 24. Augustine, *De civitate* V 26. Palladius, *Hist. Laus.* 43, 46.

[6] As the Emperor was setting out, his second wife, Galla, died in child-bed, leaving behind her Galla Placidia who was to see such grotesque adventures in the west (Zosimus IV 57; John of Antioch, fragment 187; *FHG* IV, p. 608 f.; cf. Eunapius fragment 61: *ibid.*, p. 42). The main sources for the Battle of the Frigidus are: Rufinus XI 33; Augustine, *De civitate* V 26; Orosius VII 35; Socrates V 25; Sozomen VII 24 f.; Theodoret V 24 ff.; Zosimus IV 58—perhaps including some Eunapius. Cf. John of Antioch, fragment 187. There are a number of scattered references in Claudian and Ambrose; the main ones are cited below. If W. Hartke (*Klio* XLV, 1940, pp. 104–12, cf. *Rom. Kinderkaiser*) is right, it is possible that the *Vita Gord.* (16, 2) in *Historia Augusta* reflects events at the Battle of the Frigidus. The article by Seeck and Veith in *Klio* XIII (1913), pp. 451 ff., and the full treatment in the standard histories make it un-necessary for us here to go into military and other details.

Eugenius seems to have stood on the defensive, intending perhaps to hold the Julian Alps. Theodosius won the first of the passes and in an engagement Nicomachus Flavian was defeated and committed suicide in the old Roman fashion. The Emperor left Aemona and began to make for Aquileia. The main body of the enemy confronted him in a valley by the River Frigidus, while, unknown to him, a considerable force under Arbitio was sent to take him in the rear. The prestige and the money bags of the Byzantine Emperor, not for the last time, came to the rescue, and Arbitio was bribed into joining Theodosius' side. However, Theodosius' Gothic allies had lost several thousand men.

Since things had gone so badly for him, Theodosius turned the more avidly to prayer. He was clearly outfought and outgeneralled. The historians differ in their details about the prayer. Rufinus puts the prayer in the day during the battle. The Emperor stood on a mound in sight of both armies and threw himself on the ground, and so enflamed his men to new courage. Orosius puts the prayer at night, and says he prayed all night. Theodoret is unable to resist the temptation to embroider. He says that the Emperor found a small place of prayer and passed the entire night in prayer to the Master of all things. About cockcrow, sleep conquered him and he seemed to see two men in white, riding on white horses, who told him to take courage, drive out fear, and at dawn to arm and muster his troops for the struggle. One was John the Evangelist and the other Philip the Apostle. (So the Christians now had their own Castor and Pollux.)

Next day the struggle was renewed. The decisive moment in the battle came when a storm arose, and a mighty wind rushed into the faces of Eugenius' men. The participants in the actual combat were obviously immediately affected by the wind physically. But yet Eugenius' men might have held, had not the moral effect of the wind blowing from their opponents' side been so devastating. As Ambrose says, the wounds to their bodies were not more serious than the wounds in their minds, for they realized God was fighting against them.[1] Claudian, writing a few years later, says that the Alps were easy to penetrate for Theodosius' army, and it did not profit the enemy in his caution to hold on to fortifications. Their defences fell and their barricades were opened. On Honorius' account, the north wind overturned the line of the enemy and

---

[1] Ambrose, *In Psalm.* XXXVI 25 (*PL* 14 col. 980). Cf. *Ep.* LXI 3: '... *tantam in proeliis divini auxilii fuisse praesentiam, ut nulli vertices montium adventus tui cursum retardarent, non hostilia arma impedimentum aliquod afferrent.*' Cf. also the *Gallican Chronicle* (*Chron. Min.* I, p. 650): '*Theodosius in Italiam transgreditur aperto dei favore conspirantibus ipsum elementis.*'

turned back the spears on their throwers. He is beloved of God for whom Aeolus releases the armed storms, for whom the ether fights and the winds come when called.[1] Leaving aside the pretty conceit by which Claudian manages to bring the worthless Honorius into something in which he played no part, it is clear that he believed that Theodosius received supernatural help, especially in the matter of the great wind. Claudian's view is of great importance for he was almost certainly a pagan. The pagans, even if they did not rush like rats to leave a sinking ship, recognized that God had fought on Theodosius' side, and presumed that this powerful deity was the Christian God whom the Emperor worshipped.

St Augustine, who here may be said to represent the fifth-century Christian view, had been told by combatants (on Eugenius' side) that the wind blowing from Theodosius' line had rendered their projectiles worse than useless. He then quotes Claudian with approval. It is not surprising to find his pupil Orosius following a similar line. It was the blowing of the *Bora* which brought Theodosius victory; pagans and Christians alike were agreed that the wind was sent by the divine powers. Since Theodosius was a Christian, and had prayed to his God for help, the victory must have been attributed by contemporaries to the God of the Christians. In their eyes, Christ had conquered.

Resistance to Theodosius collapsed, Eugenius was killed, and Arbogast, after taking to flight, committed suicide. Theodosius' mercy and generosity to his enemies, even for him, was remarkable.[2] For the second time he was ruler of the entire Roman world, undisputed and victorious. On entering Italy Theodosius appears to have written to Ambrose hinting that the Bishop had kept away from Milan because he thought that God would not support the Emperor. Ambrose explains that he left so as

---

[1] Claudian, *III cons. Honor.* 87–98:
    '. . . te propter et Alpes
invadi faciles cauto nec profuit hosti
munitis haesisse locis; spes inrita valli
concidit et scopulis patuerunt claustra revulsis.
te propter gelidis Aquilo de monte procellis
obruit adversas acies revolutaque tela
vertit in auctores et turbine reppulit hastas.
o nimium dilecte deo, cui fundit ab antris
Aeolus armatas hiemes, cui militat aether
et coniurati venuint ad classica venti.'

[2] Claudian, *IV cons. Honor.* 111–18; Paulinus 31; Ambrose, *Ep.* LXI 7; *De obitu Theodosii* 4. It seems to be a fair inference from Augustine, *De civitate* V 26 that some pardons to prominent people were granted on condition that they became Christian. (For comments see Seeck's edition of Symmachus, p. lix, and Alföldi, *A Festival of Isis*, p. 41.) It is only just to Christianity to point out that by the laws of war they had forfeited their lives and on their becoming Christian, contrary to Roman custom, they were spared.

to avoid having to meet Eugenius.[1] His letter reveals that where others would have ordered the building of arches of triumph, Theodosius had ordered the preparation of an offering to God, and had desired an oblation and thanksgiving to the Lord to be celebrated by the priests. Ambrose had felt that he was unworthy, and so had taken the Emperor's letter to the altar, placed it there, and held it in his hand when he offered, so that Theodosius' faith might speak in his voice, and the imperial letter might perform the office of the sacerdotal oblation.

When Ambrose came to Aquileia, Theodosius threw himself at the episcopal feet and testified that his (Ambrose's) merits and prayers had been his salvation.[2] Having made allowance for Paulinus' magnification of Ambrose, we can readily imagine the impulsive Theodosius abasing himself before Ambrose, the veritable *persona* of western episcopacy in that century. Theodosius abstained *a consortio sacramentorum* till he felt the divine grace in the safe arrival of his children.[3] Theodosius' victory was celebrated by no less a saint than Paulinus of Nola, who lauded it in a Panegyric 'Concerning victory over tyrants', pointing out that victory was rather in faith and prayer than in arms.[4]

Theodosius' victory in itself revoked the concessions made to paganism by the previous regime, and extended to the west his legislation for the last few years, but he probably inaugurated the anti-pagan policy officially and formally in the west. Zosimus says that Theodosius went to Rome, and before he left he called together the Senate (who adhered staunchly to the old religion and could not be persuaded to contemn the gods) and exhorted them to turn away from their former error, as he called it, and take to the Christian faith, which promised to remit every sin and all impiety. When he saw that none was persuaded to leave the customs which they had inherited, and which had been their guide for over a thousand years, during which time the City was unconquered, he told them that the rites and sacrifices cost too much and the expense could not be spared, nor could he commend these practices. He had therefore decided to abolish them.[5]

Prudentius says that after Theodosius had twice been a victor and twice slain tyrants, he beheld Rome and addressed her.[6] He then puts a noble speech in the Emperor's mouth expressing ideas which probably repre-

---

[1] *Ep.* LXI. *Ep.* LXII contains a request for mercy to the Emperor's enemies.
[2] Paulinus 31.
[3] Presumably Honorius and Serena, *De obitu Theod.* 34.
[4] Gennadius, *De scriptoribus ecclesiasticis* XLVIII, *PL* 58 col. 1086.
[5] Zosimus IV 59.
[6] *Contra Symmachum* I 410 ff.

sent the poet's view more than the monarch's. The Emperor praises the greatness of Rome, he accepts her God-given mission. He begs her to cast aside the unworthy accretions of paganism and find her true fulfilment in Christ, who led Constantine and Theodosius himself to victory. Taught by such edicts the City left her ancient errors (506 ff.). Her nobility responded to the Emperor's call. All but a minority if not already Christian, sought baptism. The poet mentions the Anicii, the Gracchi and other famous families—he says six hundred noble families came over (544 ff.). Among the people, too, only a few were left in paganism (578). The poet stresses that they came over freely, convinced by reason and their own judgment (611 ff.).

It is not at all certain that Theodosius visited Rome after his victory over Eugenius, but Zosimus and Prudentius certainly indicate that he made a great effort to bring the city to Christ. Probably no great pressure was needed to bring vast crowds over. The battle of the Frigidus had reinforced the teaching of the battle of the Milvian Bridge, and the pagans hurried to abandon a failing cause.

On 17 January 395 Theodosius the Lucky had the good fortune to die at the highest point of success and victory, before the inevitable repercussions of his own policies and the multitude of problems demanding immediate solution overtook him. The Emperor was not a young man and had seen many wars and vicissitudes, beside much pleasure and responsibility. Theodosius, the most Christian King, was perhaps promoted to the ranks of the gods on his death. He is given the title *divus* in inscriptions. Claudian gives him a place among the stars, and perhaps his body an assumption.[1]

The finest obituary was that uttered by Ambrose at the service held in Milan, before the body was carried to its rest at Constantinople, where it was to remain undisturbed till the coming of the Fourth Crusade in 1204.[2] Now forty days after the death they are holding lamentation just as Joseph lamented his father. Theodosius, like Jacob, supplanted the perfidy of tyrants, he put out of sight the images of the gentiles, their worship and ceremonies (4). The faith of Theodosius produced victories. Once when the soldiers there present could not engage the enemy because of their numbers and the narrowness of the country, Theodosius jumped

---

[1] *CIL* VI.1730 f., 1783, de Rossi, *Inscriptiones christianae urbis Romae*, Rome, 1861, I, p. 338. Cf. Leo, *Ep.* C, *PL* 54 col. 972. Claudian, *III cons. Honor.* 162–88. These themes and the Theodosian cult of victory are treated in detail by the writer in *There's such divinity doth hedge a King*.

[2] *De obitu Theodosii*, *PL* 16 col. 1385 ff., also ed. Mannix, Washington, 1925.

from his horse and encouraged them with the cry 'Where is the God of Theodosius?' Therefore his faith was their victory (7, 8). Theodosius was pious, merciful, faithful. His faith meant that power did not puff him up, nor did pride make him elevate himself, but his piety made him humble (12). He was always ready to forgive (13). St Ambrose compares Theodosius and his sons with some of the Old Testament kings (15 and 16). He then takes up the words of *Dilexi quoniam*[1] and applies them to the Emperor. Theodosius has loved and fulfilled the law (17–19). Like the Apostle he has fought a good fight and obtained a crown (20 and 23). When he had sinned, Theodosius humbled himself; now he turns unto his rest (28). Because he loved the Lord his God, he has earned the company of the holy. St Ambrose prays that God may grant rest to his servant Theodosius, the rest which he has prepared for his holy ones. He asks that God may turn his soul thither whence it descended (36). Now among the holy he meets Constantine, Gratian, Flaccilla, his children and his father. Maximus and Eugenius in the inferno illustrate the dangers of taking arms against the Prince. Now Theodosius is King indeed (39, 40).

Four years after his death, on Blessed Theodosius' day, St John Chrysostom preached about him.[2] He said that no ordinary duty was owed to the Blessed Theodosius, not because he was a king, but because he was pious, not because he wore a purple robe, but because he put on Christ and the weapons of the Christian warrior. With these weapons he overthrew the tyrants. When Theodosius' men were being routed, he leapt from his horse, placed his shield on the ground, knelt down and called for aid from heaven. He made the place of battle the place of a church, making war not with bows and arrows but with tears and prayers. So there befell a sudden onrush of wind, and the missiles of the foe were carried against those that discharged them. The enemy when they saw this, changed, and proclaimed him King, handing over their own King with his hands tied behind his back. The Blessed Theodosius returned renowned not only because of the Victory, but because of the manner of the victory. The soldiers did not share in the trophy with him, the whole belonged to his faith. For this reason they called him 'Blessed', nor say that he is dead.

It is true that his work, for good and for ill, is not dead.

---

[1] Psalm 116. The description of St Helena's Invention of the Cross (41–51) may be part of another homily. The oration proper resumes at *cap.* 52.
[2] *Hom. in ecclesia apostolorum, PG* 63 col. 491 f.

CONCLUSION

In his directing of the relationship between Church and State Theodosius seems to have staggered from side to side, from the totalitarian view that the State is supreme, to a dualistic view that Church and State exist side by side, and then back again. He even at one time seemed to incline towards the totalitarian view with the Church on top. But this is to mistake him. He had been brought up a western catholic of his day. He had not been born in the purple nor had he worn it before he had dealings with the Church. He took it for granted that he should assist the Church with every means at his disposal. It was not his fault that the Church was grievously divided and did not always know her own mind. He did not at any time impose his will as such on the Church; everything he did with regard to religion was in keeping with the views of a substantial and important group of bishops. In fact Theodosius was the first major exponent in policy of the *'imperator filius ecclesiae'* concept, a concept which was not without its importance in history and which in a modified form has its relevance for good or for ill today.[1]

Few men since Theodosius have been able to exert so decisive an influence over the Church Universal. Theodosius had confirmed Christianity in her career as a religion of victory in battle. By his victory at the Frigidus he had set the seal on what was begun at the Milvian Bridge. There are some who would ask whether victory on the battlefield was the victory promised by Christ who himself conquered by suffering and refused to resort to force of arms. What was to happen when victory went to Islam?

The Christians say it was their Master's last command to make disciples of all nations. It is difficult to make any estimate of numbers but there can be no doubt that under Theodosius a tremendous mass movement unto Christianity took place.[2] Those who have seen 'rice-christianity' at close quarters are the most hesitant to express an opinion about such movements.

With Theodosius' help the Nicene faith became the norm of orthodoxy and remains such to this day. If, as seems almost certain, the Niceno-Constantinopolitan Creed was accepted and ratified by the Council of 381, we owe in part to Theodosius one of the cornerstones of the Oecumenical Church. Thanks to him a schism between east and west which

---

[1] For the dangers of a too friendly government see M. A. C. Warren, *Caesar the Beloved Enemy*, London, 1955.
[2] But see *RAC* II, pp. 1139 ff. and the works of Roland Allen, also D. McGavran, *The Bridges of God*, London, 1955.

might have taken a long time to heal was brought to an end within a generation. From all this we must not suppose that what churchmen need to cause them to agree quickly on faith and order is someone with the power of a Theodosius to bang their heads together and force them to come to terms! It is too easy to exaggerate the extent to which he employed coercion in his oecumenical settlement, but it has to be admitted that he used some force. His oecumenical settlement was a fine achievement but it was partly brought about by ignoring or sweeping aside the expressed opinions over who was legitimate Bishop of Antioch of great Churches like those of Rome and Alexandria. When his successors imitated him and imposed oecumenical settlements, they were not as skilful or successful as Theodosius. But do skill and success justify, or failure and clumsiness condemn?

Once it was decided that the Nicene belief was the hallmark of orthodoxy, some decision had to be made about those who refused to agree and taught beliefs in contradiction. In theory Theodosius and his contemporaries knew the most Christian answer was to overcome heretics by love and patient discussion and by showing them the superiority of orthodox belief and life. But the use of force as an instrument of church government was by now taken for granted. It had crept in unobtrusively under Constantine, no one had raised the alarm at the time and by his sons' days it was too late. Both Nicenes and Arians had liberally used it; St Athanasius and St Cyril used it freely against their opponents. The bodies of members of the opposition to Pope Damasus had strewed the floors of a Roman basilica. In such times as these, had he not used force, so one could argue, Theodosius would have been failing in his duty. He believed, as his laws and coins show, that he was entrusted with power by God and that he knew which belief pleased heaven. Other views offended and had to be put down by every means available. Heretics were enemies of God. God had given him power; unless he smote God's enemies, how could he expect God to smite his enemies in battle? Many who were wavering would be brought to the true faith; many already self-consigned to perdition would turn back. Surely, he stood in a great succession of those who had combated heresy to protect the Church and to save the heretics—Irenaeus, Hippolytus, Epiphanius, Theodosius. He was the first of them to be in a position to use the sword rather than the pen.

We cannot in the circumstances entirely condemn Theodosius; rather perhaps one should praise him for the moderation with which he used his powers against the main body of those he had termed heretic. If we compare his measures with those of Decius and Diocletian against the

Christians or of Constantius against the Nicenes, we find that Theodosius' policy was mild. Also his bark was far worse than his bite. Socrates
says that Theodosius persecuted none of the heretics except Eunomius
because this man gathered together meetings in houses in the city.
Theodosius sent him into exile. Of the others, he molested none, nor
coerced them into communion. Sozomen, who had obviously studied
Theodosius' legislation against heretics, sums up the penalties imposed,
and adds that these were not in every case put into effect. The Emperor
did not want to punish those beneath his sway, but to intimidate them, so
that they came to the same mind as himself when thinking of things
religious.[1] But even allowing for the spirit of his age and his moderation, it
is amazing how little Theodosius and the great churchmen of his day
paused to count the cost. A general coarsening of moral fibre and lowering
of standards is bound to overtake a society whose hierarchy rub shoulders
with and use the methods of public executioners and soldiers, a society
in which many are members merely by constraint. Moreover, the pit dug
for another often receives one's own carcase, so the cynic may be excused
his smile when he finds Huneric applying Theodosius' laws to those who
were heretical in his lands, that is, the catholics.

The same basic assumption which made Theodosius desire to eliminate heresy meant that logically he would turn against Jews, Manichaeans,
apostates and pagans. In his attitude to the Jews, however, Theodosius
was most just and enlightened except when over the Callinicum affair
he was forced to do them an injustice.[2] Perhaps because of their Persian
connections the Emperor turned with unsurpassed fury on the Manichaeans and launched his every weapon against them. He was perfectly
right in believing that Manichaeism was one of the subtlest spiritual
enemies the Church has ever faced, but threats, vituperation and penalties,
including even death, are hardly the way to meet such enemies.

Constantine and Constantius had legislated against Christians who
became Jews. Here again, as was often the case, it was left for Theodosius
to take the logical last step and attack apostates from Christianity to
paganism. For us it is axiomatic that a man cannot be freely exercising his
choice of a given persuasion unless it is open to him to turn and follow
another. For Theodosius and his contemporaries it was a natural corollary
of imperial policy that since Christianity and citizenship went together,
the man who renounced the first lost the second. Moreover, a man who
had once been admitted to the truth was a culpable criminal if he

[1] Socrates V 20; Sozomen VII 12.
[2] On his policy towards the Jews, see Appendix D.

preferred a lie. Would not the apostasy of one member involve the whole body politic in a kind of whoredom if it went unpunished? Perhaps the laws against apostates retained many inside the Christian pale. Certainly the punishment of apostates has been one of the most effective means of preventing Christian missions having much numerical success in Muslim lands, and Communism may have to protect itself against the gospel in the same way.

Whatever may have been the logic of the situation, Theodosius did not attack paganism at first. Constantine had accepted Christ and wanted all his subjects to believe as he believed, but it was not practical to go ahead very quickly. Constantius made the mistake of hurrying too much, and the Julianic reaction took place; Jovian, Valentinian and Valens had to go slow. Theodosius inherited their policy, and however much he may have wished to destroy paganism, during the first decade of his reign the time was not ripe. He was able to let subordinates make tentative efforts to undermine the edifice of paganism, but he himself remained officially neutral. In the meantime, he was putting the finishing touches to the structure of the Christian state. In 392 he himself turned to the work of moving out from his entrenched position. At the Frigidus he blew the trumpet, the walls of paganism collapsed, and the Christian state, the *civitas dei* as conceived of by Eusebius and the Christian Emperors, was revealed, standing in all its grandeur and hollowness.

So then we have before us the Theodosian formula in full. First, orthodoxy is defined. Then heretics within the group are eliminated. Members of surrounding groups are made to conform or are destroyed. On all sides the weak, the indifferent and the undecided are brought into line. Before him others had been on the verge of full discovery, after him many used his technique. The Byzantine state was explicitly based on the Theodosian model. Imitations, conscious or unconscious, abound in history—in the England of the Restoration, in General Franco's Spain, let alone in countries where the same system is adopted but some other 'orthodoxy' is substituted for the Nicene faith. If the characteristic features can be identified early enough—a difficult task, for its qualities are both good and evil—men may be able to decide whether to reject it as some monstrous invention of the devil or to receive it as some gift of God.

APPENDICES

A

Two Notes on the Council of 381

THE COUNCIL OF 381 AND THE NICENO-CONSTANTINOPOLITAN CREED[1]

IT IS absolutely clear that the Council of Chalcedon in 451 associated this creed with the Council of 381.[2] It is also reasonably clear that it was known before 451. Firstly, it is quoted in recognizable form in Epiphanius, *Ancoratus* 118, that is, it was known in Asia Minor and its surrounds in 374. It is true that the text here depends on one rather corrupt manuscript and silly scribes were prone to insert well-known texts in place of little-known, but Dr Kelly himself refuses to use the argument that the autograph contained N not C. Secondly, a Latin form of C seems to have been known in the west before Chalcedon.[3] The Creed 'of Sardica' given in Codex Veronensis LX (58) which is clearly an early version of C, and whose connection with Antioch 379 seems to be assured, also indicates that a form of the creed was known in the east and in the west at an early date. Thirdly, there is a most interesting Creed given in the Syriac MS (BM Addit. 14,528) which according to the manuscript was translated from the Greek in A.D. 501.[4] Schwartz accepts that this manuscript gives a clear picture of a pre-Chalcedonian collection.[5] When translated back into Greek this creed is seen to be obviously a form of C but there are a sufficient number of minor differences to warrant the suggestion that we have here a recension of C other than the Chalcedonian.

[1] See especially J. N. D. Kelly, *Early Christian Creeds*, London, 1950.
[2] E. Schwartz, *Acta conciliorum oecumenicorum*, Berlin, 1933, II/1, ii pp. 78 f. (274 f.), 126 f. (322 f.), 94 f. (290 f.).
[3] A. E. Burn, 'The Old Latin Text of our Nicene Creed', *JTS* II, 1901, 102 ff. One can accept the gist of his argument while rejecting some of the circumstantial detail.
[4] F. Schulthess, 'Die syrischen Kanones der Synoden von Nicaea bis Chalcedon'. *Abh. der kgl. G. d. W. Gottingen*, phil.-hist. Kl., N.F. X 2, Berlin, 1908, p. v, and Wright's *Catalogue of Syriac MSS in the British Museum*, DCCCCVI, 1030.
[5] 'Die Kanonessammlungen der alten Reichskirche', *Zeitschrift der Savigny-Stiftung* LVI *kanon. Abt.* XXV, 1936, pp. 1–114, especially pp. 3 ff.

G

Schwartz suggested that Meletius of Antioch took a previously existing semi-Arian collection of canons and put N at the head of it. He considers however, that C, which follows N in this MS, was inserted later and that this is betrayed to us by the fact that the list of names of the Nicene fathers is separated from the creed by the insertion of C.[1] He considers that C was put beside N in Chalcedonian times, when it was accepted as a mere reinforcing of the teaching of N. Schwartz' idea that Meletius did the collecting is no more than a suggestion. All that the evidence warrants is the supposition that at about the time of the peace of the Church (379–382) a collection of canons, which could include creeds, was drawn up at Antioch. The person drawing up the collection could as easily insert C between N and the list of Nicene Fathers in 382, as his counterpart, working in 451/452.

An examination of the position of C in the Syriac MSS given by Schulthess shows a difference in its position between the MS we have been studying and BM Addit. 14,526 which is derived from a definitely post-Chalcedonian collection. In the latter the order is: Canons of Chalcedon, Chalcedon on the Faith, N, C. This is the natural post-Chalcedonian order. Our MS, with its placing of C right away from Chalcedon and close to Nicaea, surely suggests an earlier arrangement. If BM Addit. 14,528 is evidence of a pre-Chalcedonian collection, it is reasonable to suppose that the creed C it contains is pre-Chalcedonian.

The travail of biblical scholars over ascription of authorship and pseudepigraphy reminds us that the ancients did not think as we think in these matters. It seems safe to conclude that a form of C was in circulation in the Asia Minor area in the 370s, it was accepted at Antioch in 379 and at Constantinople in 381. In later days when the Council of 381 came to be ranked with Nicaea 325, it was natural that C should be associated in a special way with the Second Oecumenical Council.

THE LOCATION OF THE SEES REPRESENTED AT THE COUNCIL
(See map)

Firstly a bishop list was drawn up on the basis of the Patmian, Priscan, Isidorian, Dionysian, Syriac and Latin lists. (See *Studia Patristica*, ed. Aland and Cross, Berlin, 1957, I 635 ff., and the authorities there cited; and for the technique see H. Gelzer, 'Geog. und onomatologische Bemerkungen zu der Liste de Väter des Konzils von 381', *Byz. Zeit.*, 1903, and

[1] 'Über die Bischofslisten der Synoden von Chalkedon, Nicaea und Konstantinopel', *Abhandlungen der Bayerischen Akademie der Wissenschaften, phil.-hist. Abt.*, N.F., *Heft* 13, Munich, 1937, pp. 4 and 10. Reviewed in *Byzantion* XII, 1937, pp. 32 ff.

Patrum Nicaenorum nomina, Leipzig, 1898.) This list was compared with lists which mention some of the Fathers present. These are:

1. The Testament of St Gregory Nazianzen (*PG* 37 col. 393 f. Cf. Martroye, *M m. de la Soc. Antiq. de France* LXXVI p. 219).

2. The law XVI : 1 : 3 of 30 July 381 and Sozomen's version of it (VII 9).

3. The lists of Socrates V 8 and Theodoret V 8.

4. The lists of earlier councils, such as Nicaea 325, Seleucia 359 (Epiphanius, *Adv. haer.* III 73, *PG* 42 col. 452 f.), Antioch 363 (Socrates III 25), Antioch 379 (*Cod. Ver.* LX (58), *PL* 13 col. 354).

5. The bishops consecrated by the Meletians in 379–380 (Theodoret V 4).

Thirdly, the sites mentioned in the revised list were studied and located with the aid of A. H. M. Jones' *Cities of the East Roman Provinces*, Oxford, 1937, and W. M. Ramsay's *Historical Geography of Asia Minor*, London, 1890, and *Cities and Bishoprics of Phrygia*, 2 vols, Oxford, 1895 and 1897. The reader may also compare F. van der Meer and C. Mohrmann, *Atlas of the Early Christian World*, London, 1958. A number of sites must still be located by conjecture, and they are marked 'site', many more are located by mere probability, but the purpose of the map is to bring out the broad areas which formed the basis on which the oecumenical settlement of 381 was built.

B

The Patmian Canons[1]

AFTER GIVING the six canons attributed to Constantinople 381, the early ninth century Patmos manuscripts POB′ and POΓ′ give 21 canons which are also said to have been 'set forth in Constantinople at the time of the blessed Nectarius by the 150'. After these canons the manuscripts give the Greek bishop lists of the Council of 381 which are the most accurate we have. One cannot help thinking that since the lists are obviously genuine, so are the canons. But all of them except XVIII and XXI appear in St Basil's Third Canonical Letter to Amphilochius.[2] As Basil was to a large extent incorporating material already old, unless our canons are copying his, it is likely that the Patmian canons and his canons go back to an antecedent original.

It remains to explain the associations, if any, with the Council of 381—after all there is no evidence earlier than the superscription in these ninth-century MSS. It is possible that the scribe found them in the much older collection of Palladius of Amasia and Bishop Valerian which he mentions (bishops of those names are to be found in the list of those who attended Ephesus 431) and attributed them to the Council of 381. In that they are apparently given after the fifth and sixth canons of 381, which are more correctly attributed to 382, if they are to be associated with our period at all, it is best to attribute these canons to the Council of Constantinople of 382 when Nectarius did preside.

Possibly the canons were accepted as a penitential by a group of the bishops at Constantinople 382, and were therefore associated with the Second Oecumenical Council, but were not officially received. Some of the Councils between 325 and 381 left behind 'minority' decisions, not necessarily because the whole Council did not support them, but because coteries of bishops could easily form during a Council to transact business in between, or soon after, the main sittings. The Patmian canons may have been accepted by such a group, meeting in 382.

[1] C. H. Turner, *JTS* XV, 1914, gives a transcription of parts of the MSS, together with the most valuable comments. See also E. Schwartz, 'Kanonessammlungen der alten Reichskirche', in *Zeitschrift der Savigny-Stiftung für Rechtsgeschichte*, LVI, kanon. Abt. XXV, 1936, p. 23. He had access to a work by Beneshevich who apparently edited the MSS as a whole.

[2] *PG* 32 col. 797 ff., Canons LVI–LXXIV.

Only the canons not given by Basil need be discussed here. Canon XVIII states that all those who do not recognize theologically the homoousian Triad according to the τόμος set forth at Antioch, must be called Pneumatomachoi. The immediate implication of this seems to be that both the Council of Antioch 379 (for it is probably to the tome of that Council to which the canon is referring) and the Councils of 381/382 explicitly upheld the *homoousion* of the Holy Spirit. As for the Council of Antioch 379, our unquestionable information is so scanty that it is impossible to judge whether this canon is making a statement of fact or not. It would however seem that it may be good evidence for what Antioch 379 accepted. As for Constantinople 381, we have seen that in its officially received and related documents, in places where a statement of the *homoousion* of the Spirit would have been expected, the Council avoided such a statement. Also it has to be noted that the first undoubted canon of 382 (called 381 V) is not explicit about the *homoousion* of the Spirit. It would seem then that the Councils of 379 and 382 which were largely concerned with the problem of reunion with the west, were more prepared to give the *homoousion* to the Spirit, than Constantinople 381, which was concerned primarily with restoring peace to the eastern Church. If there is this difference between the attitudes of the Councils of 379 and 382 as against 381, it is possible that this difference is to be explained by saying that in 381 Theodosius and his advisers hoped to reconcile many of the 'Fringers' who were vague about the Third Person, but who were not Pneumatomachoi. By 382 some of the impatient younger bishops who had done so much to make Gregory Nazianzen despair, may have accepted these canons in a spirit of out-Basilling Basil.

The other canon not in Basil's collection but in the Patmos collection, is Canon XXI. It is concerned with those who make accusations on 'ghostly' charges,[1] and then in sickness or fear confess they had spoken falsely in their accusations or evidence. If this canon is to be associated with the Council of 382, it may have to do with accusations brought against bishops and clergy, and be in parallel with Canon VI (of 381) which is really the second canon of Constantinople 382, even as Patmos XVII is in parallel with Canon V (the first of 382). It adds little of importance to our study, beyond reinforcing the evidence of Canon VI that accusations against clergy had become common.

[1] ἐπὶ ψυχικοῖς ἐγκλήμασι. The second word is ambiguous: it may mean charges to do with the release of a soul from the body, that is, charges involving the possibility of death (cf. IX : 35 : 5). More probably, it may refer to charges made on the basis of alleged spiritual, i.e. ecclesiastical, offences.

C

Two Chronological Questions

THE DATING OF THE BLOOD-BATH

THERE IS today no question about the year—it was 390 (Rauschen, p. 317; Seeck, *Regesten*, p. 277). The problem is to determine the month.

If one may trust Theodoret (V 17) and accept an eight-month penance with a reconciliation at about Christmas, the massacre took place in April/May at the latest. But these details are given in no other historian, and Theodoret is notoriously prone to using his imagination to fill out details. Theodoret is clearly paralleling the case of Theodosius and Ambrose at Milan with the story of the Emperor Philip the Arab and the bishop (probably Babylas) at Antioch.[1] The reconciliation of Philip was at Easter, Theodoret could not use Easter as it was too early in the year, so he decided to use Christmas.

Some other method of dating has to be attempted. Perhaps the law IX : 7 : 6 will provide the clue required. This law against homosexuals may have some connection with the affair at Thessalonica, for Sozomen indicates that the cause of the riot was an affair of homosexuality. If so, it is not likely that the law was posterior to the affair. A case of homosexuality in Macedonia was not likely to cause the Emperor to issue a law about it in the west. Rather, if copies of it were sent to Macedonia and other parts of the Empire, one can envisage the law causing the riot. If this law is connected with the riot we may have a *terminus post quem*. But we have to fix a date for IX : 7 : 6. The subscription as it stands states that the law was promulgated on 6 August 390 at Forum Traiani. The same law appears in the *Collatio legum Mosaicarum et Romanarum* (5.3) where it is said to have been set forth on 14 May at Atrium Minervae. No consuls are given. It is possible that the law of August is a reaffirmation of the law of May. It may be suggested that this law was drawn up at Milan in early May. The copy for Thessalonica would appear there at the most only some two weeks later than the law appeared at Atrium Minervae. Allowing time for the arrest to follow the promulgation, the riot to follow the arrest and the Emperor's decision

---

[1] Eusebius, *Hist. Eccl.* VI 34. John Chrysostom, *De S. Babyla* 6 (*PG* 50 col. 541).

to be made and carried back, the massacre could hardly have taken place before mid-June at the very earliest.

The law IX : 40 : 13 may provide a *terminus ante quem*. If the super- and sub-scriptions are right, the law was sent by Gratian from Verona on 18 August 382 to Flavianus the Praetorian Prefect, and would not help our discussion here. But this law or a law very like it is clearly referred to by Rufinus (XI 18) and Sozomen (VII 25) in connection with Theodosius' repentance. Seeck and Palanque are satisfied that the law was issued in 390 and that the dating to 382 is incorrect.[1]

If IX : 40 : 13 is dated to 18 August 390, one would like to think that it indicates the date of the submission of Theodosius to the Church. Rufinus, Sozomen and Theodoret connected the law with the submission. In effect this amounts to one witness—Rufinus.[2] There is no reason other than the evidence of Theodoret to prevent the submission coinciding with the spontaneous retraction, except the fact that the Code does not indicate Theodosius' return to Milan till later, and it is taken that XVI : 3 : 1 indicates continued alienation from the Church. This last is not a necessary supposition, but the absence from Milan is an insuperable difficulty, for it is taken that Theodosius surrendered at Milan.

Theodosius was at Milan on 5 July according to XI : 16 : 18. On 18 August according to IX : 40 : 13 he was at Verona. XVI : 2 : 28 of 23 August is from Verona. His last law from Verona is XIII : 5 : 19 of 8 September. His first law from Milan was VI : 27 : 6 of 26 November. The issue of laws does not indicate an Emperor's every move. He could quite easily have been back at Milan between 23 August and 2 September but it is not likely. On the other hand, the Emperor might quite well have left Verona on 9 September. If he left Verona soon after his last law there on 8 September and returned to Milan and submitted (it is at least possible that he carried on negotiations from Verona and only returned to Milan when he was sure of reception), the pause in legislation between 8 September and 26 November would then be explained as his time of penance. As a penitent he did not wear the Imperial ornaments (Rufinus XI 18) and therefore, presumably, refrained from any legislation. He resumed legislation on 26 November and so was presumably received into communion not long before that.

[1] Seeck, *Gesch.* V, pp. 231, 532 f.; *Regesten*, pp. 116 and 92; Palanque, *Essai*, pp. 68 f. and 76; *Ambroise*, p. 230. But see also the arguments of the older historians summarized in Rauschen *ad loc.*

[2] Palanque (*Ambroise*, p. 230, note 176) says there is no connection between the law and the submission. Having accepted Theodoret's tale about Christmas he can say no other. Rufinus was probably not dependent on Gelasius of Caesarea at this point but on his own study of the legislation or local Italian tradition.

There remains for discussion one other clue to the dating. St Ambrose clearly wrote *Ep.* LI not long after the news of the massacre reached Milan, and Theodosius' revocation of his order.[1] Palanque points out that in *Ep.* LI 14, the bishop mentions '*signa caelestia*'. Palanque says that a comet appeared in 390 on 22 August and remained visible till 17 September, the letter is therefore not anterior to the earlier date.[2] If this suggestion is accepted, it indicates that the massacre took place some time before 22 August. If Theodosius submitted soon after the receipt of the letter, his submission took place after that date.[3]

It is therefore suggested that the riot took place after mid-June 390, the spontaneous retraction before 18 August and that the Emperor submitted to the Church soon after 8 September 390. He underwent penance till shortly before 26 November.

THE DATING OF THE 'PRO TEMPLIS' OF LIBANIUS AND THE FALL OF THE SERAPEUM

A safe *terminus post quem* for the Oration is easily found—Libanius twice (*capp.* 15 and 19) mentions a Christian leader called Flavian, and this is pretty clearly the Bishop of Antioch who acceded in 381. As for a *terminus ante quem*: Libanius says sacrifices continue at Alexandria (35, 44) so the Oration was written before the fall of the Serapeum. It is probable that this temple was destroyed in 391 for the following reasons:

1. Eunapius says that the cult of the gods and the temple of Serapis were destroyed in the reign of Theodosius, when Theophilus presided over the Christians, Euetius was prefect of the City, and Romanus in charge of the military.[5] The law XVI : 10 : 11 has an uncommon dual address to Evagrius, the Augustal Prefect, and Romanus, Count of

---

[1] See especially *Ep.* LI 6. Cf. Palanque, *Ambroise*, p. 583.

[2] But see also the arguments of McGuire in *Catholic Historical Review*, 1934, pp. 316 f.

[3] It is not necessary here to discuss the customs of the Western Church in regard to length of penance, since the enormity of Theodosius' crime and his high rank presented no real analogy which would provide a precedent to guide St Ambrose in his decision as to how long a penance to impose.

[4] Besides the standard works by Rauschen and Seeck, see also Gothofredus, *Opera juridica minora*, Leyden, 1733, and his edition of *Pro Templis* with notes, 1634, pp. 469 ff.; Tillemont, *Histoire*, note 16 on Theodosius (*tome* V, pp. 734 ff.); G. R. Sievers, *Das Leben des Libanius*, Berlin, 1868, p. 192; R. Förster's edition of Libanius, vol. III, pp. 80 f.; van Loy, *Byzantion* VIII, 1933, 11–19; P. Petit, *ibid.* XXI, pp. 285–310, *Libanius et la vie municipale à Antioche au IVe siècle*; R. A. Pack, *Studies in Libanius*.

[5] *Vitae philosophorum et sophistarum*: Boissonade, pp. 43 f., Didot, pp. 472 f.

Egypt, and was sent on 16 June 391 from Aquileia. It seems reasonable to suppose that Euetius is a mistake for Evagrius. It seems likely that Eunapius knew of the law, and connects the sending of the law with the destruction of the temple.

2. 391 as the date is indicated also by Sozomen (VII 15), who says Romanus was in charge of troops and Evagrius prefect of Alexandria. This links up with the address of XVI : 10 : 11 of 16 June 391. In that the title of Evagrius is not exactly the same as that given in the law, we may take it that Sozomen is here an independent authority.

3. St Jerome, writing his *De viris illustribus* in Palestine in 392, mentions that Sophronius had written a book about the overthrow of this temple (*cap.* 134).

4. 391 is also the date indicated by the Gallican Chronicle (*Chron. Min.* I, p. 650) which puts the fall of the Serapeum in the eighth year after the death of Gratian.

5. On the other hand Marcellinus Comes records the destruction under 389. His chronology is not so accurate that one can accept his evidence in the face of the other witnesses.

We may conclude then that so much of the evidence points to 391 as the date for the fall of the Serapeum, that it makes this date almost a certainty.

Apart from the fall of the Serapeum providing a *terminus ante quem* in 391 for the Oration, this year can be shown to be this *terminus* in that Libanius (33) makes much of the continuance of sacrifice at Rome, and this probably came to an end (for the moment) in 391 as a result of XVI : 10 : 10 of 24 February 391.

It is clear then that the *Pro Templis* reflects the conditions of the early and perhaps middle years of Theodosius' reign, and can be adduced as evidence for them. It remains to be seen whether its dating can be more accurately fixed: to do this it is necessary to examine a few of the possible pieces of evidence as they occur in the text of the *Pro Templis*.

Libanius refers to the greatness of the honours with which the Emperor has honoured him (*Or.* XXX 1; cf. XLV 1). It is known from Eunapius[1] that later Emperors (that is, later than Julian) offered Libanius an honorary prefecture. Seeck (*Gesch.* V, pp. 527 f.) takes it that Libanius, in the passages cited, is referring to this Prefecture and he links it up with chapter 258 of the *Vita*, which is fairly securely datable to 388. Therefore, he takes it, the *Pro Templis* is after 388. Libanius never him-

---

[1] *Vitae phil. et soph.*: Boissonade, pp. 99 f., Didot, p. 496. Eunapius says he refused the honour.

self unequivocally refers to this Prefecture, and Tillemont's characteristic labelling of it as a fable may well be the true answer (*Hist.* V, p. 733). If we compare this passage with *Or.* XXXVII 7, it is clear that it does not refer to an official title conferred on Libanius, but to a favour granted in connection with the inheritance of his illegitimate son Cimon. Sufficient has been said to show that Libanius' Prefecture is not a secure basis on which to date the *Pro Templis* after 388.

In Chapter 13 Libanius asks what are the actions of the monks other than warring in time of peace against the farmers. The mention of peace would indicate that the bulk of the raids against the pagans took place before the war against Maximus, which brought the unbroken period of peace since the settlement with the Goths to an end. He goes on to say that it is more dreadful that those who were naturally their allies in trouble should make them suffer in a time of quietness. The reference to alliance is probably to the intercession of the monks during the *stasis* at Antioch in early 387. It would seem then that the Oration was written after the *stasis* in spring 387.

Later in the Oration Libanius says that the Emperor has not shut out pagans but has given them positions of power, has eaten with them, and this often; and now in addition, he has yoked with himself, thinking it profitable for the kingdom, a man who confesses the gods both before others and before him (53). If the yoking together indicates an appointment to the Praetorian Prefectship, this may be a reference to Tatian's promotion. In this case the Oration dates from after spring 388 when Tatian was made Praetorian Prefect. Another point which supports this dating, is that the escapades of the monks in the east took place at a time when high authorities were willing either to wink at or support them. This suggests a time either after late 390 (which is unlikely since it is so close to the fall of the Serapeum), or before Tatian came to power (spring 388). There also seems to be a good deal of cogency in the argument that the *Pro Templis* could not have been written until after the death of Cynegius had brought the pagan Tatian to office. It is true that the Oration was probably for private circulation but Libanius would run no risks.

Arguments from silence can seldom stand by themselves, but it is noticeable that there is no indication of Theodosius' victory over Maximus. This would have been grist to the orator's mill. The same can be said about Libanius' silence concerning Theodosius' benevolence towards paganism during his visit to Rome in 389.

We may conclude then that the Oration was written after 381 and before 391. Most of the indications of time point to the latter half of the period.

The Oration is first-hand evidence for the policy of Theodosius towards paganism for about the first ten years of his reign. To go a little beyond absolute certainty, it may be suggested that the work dates from fairly soon after the death of Cynegius and before the victory over Maximus, perhaps in the early summer of 388.

D

Notes on Certain Types of Legislation

THE LAWS REGARDING SUNDAY

FROM HER earliest days the Church celebrated Sunday week by week in commemoration of the Lord's resurrection. It was natural that when men with Christian convictions came to rule over the Roman Empire, they should order that this day should be observed as a day on which no legal business was to be carried on.

Theodosius did not enact anything outstanding in this matter, so it is only necessary to describe briefly the laws issued on the subject between 379 and 395, and to place them in their context as continuations of the policies of previous Emperors. On 3 November 386 Valentinian II ordered that on the day of the Sun, which the elders rightly called the Lord's day, all litigation, all business and all legal meetings and collection of debts were to cease.[1] Constantine had forbidden legal business on Sundays, with the exception of such desirable acts as emancipation and manumission (II : 8 : 1 of 321). Constantine's law, on the face of it, celebrated Sunday more for the sake of Sol than of Christ. Valentinian I ordered that no Christian was to be summoned by tax-collectors on a Sunday since it was an auspicious day (VIII : 8 : 1). Valentinian II's law therefore goes beyond any previous enactment, and the Christian associations of Sunday are made quite clear.

Theodosius' law *Nullus omnino* may be dated with equal probability to either 386 or 394.[2] Theodosius stated that no judge was to take time off for plays, circus shows or wild animal chases except on the natal and accession days of the Emperors. Even on these he was to attend only in the morning and not return after lunch. No one was to give a spectacle on Sunday, nor disturb divine worship by producing an artificial solemnity. Theodosius was legislating against the neglect of their proper duties by judges. The Emperor also intended that people should attend church, and not have to face the temptation of going to the spectacles instead.

In his law issued at Rome in 389 regarding public holidays and court days, Theodosius included Sunday as a day on which there was to be no

---

[1] II : 8 : 18. XI : 7 : 13 and VIII : 8 : 3 are versions of the same law.
[2] XV : 5 : 2, see Seeck, *Regesten*, pp. 284 and 94.

business (II : 8 : 19). In 392 he ordered that on the festival days of the Sun, the contests of the circus were to be prohibited. On these days no gatherings for spectacles were to interfere with the venerable mysteries of the Christian law. When the natal day of the Emperor fell on a Sunday, it was to be celebrated as usual (II : 8 : 20). Theodosius' interest does not seem to have been so much the stopping of the games and other activities on Sundays, as the preventing of counter-attractions to church services. It is possible that the Puritan inherits his Sunday from Theodosius.

THEODOSIUS' EASTER LEGISLATION

It was the custom of the Roman Emperors to grant amnesties at times of national rejoicing. It was natural that Christian Emperors should choose Easter as one of the festive days on which prisoners should be released. Thus Valentinian I ordered that all those who were shut in prison were to be released—'*ob diem paschae, quem intimo corde cele-bramus*'. Those accused of treason, of crime against the dead, of poisoning, using magic, of adultery, rape or homicide were excepted.[1]

While still at Thessalonica in March 380 Theodosius sent a law to the Vicarius of Macedonia ordering that during the forty days which preceded the paschal time, all trials and inquiries were forbidden (IX : 35 : 4). During the same year or the next, Theodosius granted an amnesty out of reverence for the feast of Easter to prisoners with the exception of those guilty of the five crimes.[2] Like Valentinian I before him, Theodosius reverenced Easter and wished to release captives, except those accused of very serious crimes.

In 381 Gratian also published an Easter amnesty. Among the exceptions, he mentions those who had spoken against the Emperor, who had killed relations or committed homicide, adultery, rape, incest, made poison for soul or body, or counterfeited the divine features of the Emperors. The amnesty was for first offenders only (IX : 38 : 6). Valentinian II in his Easter amnesty of 384 granted freedom to those accused of lighter crime, but maintained the exceptions which by this time had become almost customary (*lex* 7). A year later he ordered that release for all was to be automatic when Easter came. He added the usual exceptions with the addition of men guilty of sacrilege and tomb robbery (*lex* 8).

---

[1] IX : 38 (*De indulgentiis criminum*) : 3 of 367 or 369. Cf. *lex* 4 of 368 or 370. These laws prove conclusively Valentinian's personal Christianity.

[2] *Constit. Sirm.* VII. This law is not dated. Eutropius to whom it is addressed was Praetorian Prefect of the East in 380/381 (Rauschen, pp. 63, 86). The five crimes were homicide, adultery (incest), rape, poisoning, treason. See also IX : 38 : 2 (by Constantius).

The provisions of this law can hardly have become the rule, for laws containing Easter amnesties continued to be published.

In 386 Theodosius issued an Easter amnesty which would be better described as a joyful oration than a law (*Sirm.* VIII). As Easter approached the Emperor could say that beside the clemency which had been laid down and passed on by his ancestors, he had exercised his sacred mind in a deep effusion of humanity. Throughout the time between the venerable and festal days he released from chains, brought back from exile, there was hardly a day on which he did not order something merciful and holy—he himself suffered a certain loss of time if no one needed liberation. (Cf. Suetonius, *Titus* VIII.) So he wished to relax the laws as far as possible, and ordered an amnesty. He then gives some exceptions of the usual kind, and explains why these criminals must be excepted. Apart from the cause of the rejoicing being Easter, there is nothing in this law which a pagan could not have said with equal sincerity. 'Philanthropy' was common to both religions, and the means of ensuring it were much the same. In his *Homilies on the Statues*, which he preached in 387, St John Chrysostom nowhere reveals a knowledge of this particular law, but he speaks of an Easter amnesty in which Theodosius said he wished that he could bring the dead to life again (*Hom.* XXI 2). We may suppose that Easter amnesties were greater in number even than those which survive.

In 389 Theodosius mentioned the holy days of the Pascha among the official holidays (II : 8 : 19). Shortly after the publication of this law, Theodosius ordered that there was to be no punishment inflicted on the body in which the release of the spirit could be expected during the sacred days of the Quadragesima period (IX : 35 : 5). In 392 he ordered that all acts, that is legal business, whether public or private, were to be kept apart from the fifteen days of the Pascha (II : 8 : 21). This law in effect coincides with the provisions of the law of 389 which granted seven days before and after Easter (II : 8 : 19).

In this sphere of legislation too Theodosius maintained and continued with some heightening, a tradition received from his predecessors.

RELIGIOUS LAWS TO DO WITH THE 'CURIALES'[1]

Since the reforms of Diocletian and Constantine, the *curiales* had been left with few powers and privileges, but many expenses and responsibilities. To maintain their system of local government, public entertain-

---

[1] Recently Petit's study (*Libanius et la vie municipale à Antioche*) has shed a good deal of light on this subject. It is not possible to be certain to what extent the muni-

ment and tax-collecting, the Emperors had to keep up the number of these men. In 320 or 326 Constantine therefore ordered that no decurion was after that date to join the clergy (XVI : 2 : 3). When Constantius II in 361 freed bishops from curial liability, he added that if *curiales* had become clergy of a rank below bishop, they too might be freed if the *curia* consented and if they were men of personal sanctity and the people wished it. If these conditions were not fulfilled, these clergy were to hand over their goods to their children, and if they had no children, two-thirds of their property was to be given to relations, or the *curia*, and their obligations fulfilled (XII : 1 : 49).

Julian ordered Christian decurions to be recalled (XII : 1 : 50 of 362). Valentinian and Valens reached a compromise. Valentinian ordered in 364 that if a decurion wished to serve in the Church he was to hand over his property to a relation or to the *curia*. In 370 it was ordered that if a *curialis* had spent ten years in the clergy he was free, and was to retain his possessions (XII : 1 : 59 and XVI : 2 : 19). Presumably the underlying rule was that on entry into the clergy a decurion handed over his property, but a man's ministry was not to be haunted by endless possibilities of claims upon him. The first part of this principle was confirmed by Gratian in 383 (XII : 1 : 99).

In November 383 Theodosius ordered that *curiales* who preferred to serve the churches rather than the municipalities had to leave their property behind. It is probably with sincerity that he adds that it is not fitting that minds bound to the divine service should be occupied with desires for patrimonies (XII : 1 : 104). This too is a confirmation of the old principle, which was reiterated in laws of 385 and 386 (VIII : 5 : 46 and XII : 1 : 115).

It was also in 386 that Theodosius sent XII : 1 : 112 to Egypt. In obtaining a High Priesthood he was to be the stronger candidate who had devoted more to his home town and had not departed from the cult of the temples through the observance of Christianity. (As far as this the law might be by Julian!) It was not right that temples and the solemnities of temples should involve those whose minds had been imbued with the true principle of divine religion, and who ought to flee from such an office, even if it were not prohibited to them. The *archierosyne* here refers to the provincial High Priesthood, which entailed oversight of temples and

cipalities were Christian. They are usually considered to have remained mainly pagan. But Christianity was likely to spread widely in this class of society, as it did in the others. Decurions would probably gain to some extent by the ending of paganism, if they were relieved of their duty of keeping certain temples in repair. It is dangerous to conclude too facilely that the municipalities were bulwarks of paganism.

games. It was probably an expensive duty which bore heavily on its bearer, but it was one of the highest honours which crowned the career of a *curialis* who had fulfilled his duties to his city. At the moment the holding of this position, as the law itself suggests, involved the High Priest in rites in which a Christian could not conscientiously participate. Later on some High Priesthoods became secular offices in connection with the Christianized Emperor cult.[1]

If we take it that Theodosius was intent on the ruin of paganism, it is possible to interpret this law along those lines. We may say that everyone knew that people wanted to avoid this ruinous office, and now it is laid down, under show of protecting paganism, that the Christian may not undertake the rôle. If this interpretation is near the truth, from the point of view of civic patriotism, it is indeed a sad day when long service to the *patria* is rewarded by an office which leads to certain financial ruin, and when by implication a Christian, since he cannot serve temples, cannot be a good citizen.

Against this interpretation it may be said that so far as one can make out, Theodosius did not want to ruin the municipalities. Secondly, it may be said that the holding of a provincial High Priesthood entailed great honour and some considerable privileges. Not every *curialis* was as lacking in civic pride as those who tried to escape their duties by becoming senators or Christian clergy. Thirdly, the Emperor's concern seems to be to protect Christians from being involved in pagan rites; he is not really considering the possible effects on paganism.

In a law of 390 (XII : 1 : 121) Theodosius laid down that any *curiales* who had become clergy more than two years before were to be free of curial obligations. This was indeed generous, for Ambrose knew cases where men who had served forty years were being troubled (*Ep.* XL 29).

In the following year by XII : 1 : 123 he renewed this law but pointed out that fathers who were not permitted to leave their place of origin could not set their sons free from obligation. The sons of clergy were to serve the *curia* with their father's estates, unless they already held a place in the Church.

It is possible that Theodosius would have liked to have been more generous. The iron grip of financial exigency gave continuity to the curial policies of the Emperors from Diocletian onwards.

---

[1] E. Beurlier, *Le Culte impérial*, Paris, 1891, pp. 296 ff. On the disapproval of the Church of Christians undertaking these duties, see Duchesne, 'Le Concile d'Elvire et les flamines chrétiens' (*Mélanges Renier*, 1886, pp. 159 ff.). We may also compare the dilemma of West African Christians when enstooled as Chiefs.

CLERICAL PRIVILEGES AND RIGHTS OF ASYLUM[1]

Early in the reign the Emperor granted that guardians of churches and holy places and persons carrying out religious functions were to be exempt from the poll tax (XVI : 2 : 26 of 381).

So far as disputes between clerics were concerned, Theodosius maintained that the civil courts, including the Emperor's, could not take cognizance. 'They have their own judges and nothing is in common between them and the secular laws so far at least as ecclesiastical cases are concerned, which ought to be decided by episcopal authority' (*Sirm.* III of 384; cf. Canon VI of Constantinople). He also asserted that bishops were not to be compelled to give testimony (XI : 39 : 8 of 381). Presbyters might give testimony without being tortured, but litigators could take action against them for perjury if it was suspected that they had suppressed the truth. Clergy below the rank of presbyter were to be heard as the laws prescribed (XI : 39 : 10 of 385 or 386).

During 392 Theodosius issued certain laws relating to the Church's right to protect criminals. He ordered that the sentence of any person found guilty of serious crime was to be carried out even if the person had been sheltered by the clergy or had made an appeal. Any official who did not resist interference of this kind was to be severely punished (IX : 40 : 15). A month later he commanded that in cases of such convicted criminals the process of law was not to be held up by appeals or by the intervention of any of the bishops, clergy or people (XI : 36 : 31). As a background to these laws we may compare what St Ambrose says on the subject in his *De officiis* (II . xxi . 102). He indicates that the clergy can gain regard by rescuing a poor man from the grip of a strong man, or a man condemned to death—if it can be done without commotion and ostentation. St Ambrose, very reasonably, points out that it must be done out of pity, and not if the criminal deserves his punishment. St Ambrose would in fact have agreed that the Emperor's laws were just. The laws and St Ambrose's words suggest that the clergy were interfering to rescue condemned criminals quite regardless of the justice of their condemnation. Unless this practice were brought under proper control the whole edifice of criminal justice would be undermined.

On October 18 Theodosius gave permission for public debtors to be

---

[1] We have to bear in mind that Theodosius was dealing with particular cases and we do not know the *Sitz im Leben*. For the general background see '*Audentia Episcopalis*' in *RAC* I, pp. 915 ff. and G. Lardé, *Le Tribunal du clerq*, Paris, 1920. Also 'Asylrecht', *RAC* I, pp. 836 ff.; 'Droit d'asile', *DACL* IV, pp. 1549 ff.; *PW* II 2, 1879 ff.; Martroye in *Mém. soc. nat. antiq. de France* LXXV (1919), pp. 159 ff. and Hess, *Canons of Sardica*, pp. 131 ff. Cf. also IX : 44 : 1.

drawn from the churches if they fled to them, or the bishops who were proved to be hiding them could be made to pay out on their behalf. In the future no debtor was to be defended by the clergy, or otherwise the clergy were to pay the debt of one whom they believed should be defended (IX : 45 : 1). This is the first law to mention the Church's right of asylum. Presumably criminals and debtors of all kinds had, till the time of this law, been able to seek asylum in any church and remain unmolested. This law restricts that right in the case of public debtors, but it admits that the Church has a right of asylum. Theodosius' attitude of respect for the clergy had perhaps somewhat abated since his early days, more probably once again we may suppose that the financial exigencies of the state overruled the personal religious views of the Emperor.

LAWS REGULATING CHURCH LIFE

Theodosius did not hesitate to regulate the life of the Church where lack of discipline was affecting the secular world.

In a long and complicated law of 390 the Emperor ordered that in accordance with the Apostle's precept no woman, unless she were full sixty years of age and had offspring at home, was to join the fellowship of deaconesses.[1] Her goods were to go in trust to her children (if they were minors) though the woman herself was to have full power over the income of her estates during her lifetime. She was not to consume any of the splendid things of a noble household under the pretext of religion. At her death she was not to appoint any church or cleric or poor man as her heir. The Emperor made provision against attempts by such devices as death-bed extortions and secret trusteeships to circumvent the law. He then stated that women who cut off their hair as an act of devotion were to be kept away from the church doors and the altars. A bishop who permitted such a woman to enter was to be deposed and no excuse would save him (XVI : 2 : 27).

The provisions regarding women being sixty before entering the ministry of widows or deaconesses and about shaving the head, are in keeping with the Church's own laws.[2] It is the regulation about bequests to clerics which appears to be new. We may however compare XVI : 2 : 20

---

[1] '*Cui votiva domi proles sit*', literally '*to whom there is the desired progeny at home*'. It is difficult to understand whether the '*nisi*' governs this—*Cod. Just.*, 1 : 3 : 9 omits it. Sozomen (VII 16) writes, εἰ μὴ παῖδας ἔχοιεν. The meaning seems to be that she must be over sixty and have heirs at home.

[2] On the age of women becoming widows or deaconesses see I Tim. 5.9 (the apostolic precept) and Chalcedon, Canon XV. Phoebe (Rom. 16.1–2) and Pliny's *ministrae* (*Ep.* X 96) appear to be young women. St Ambrose (*De viduis*, PL 16 col. 247 ff.) envisages young women joining the order. His difficulty, unlike Theodosius', was to

of Valentinian I to Damasus in 370 in which he forbade ecclesiastics to receive money from rich Roman women, widows or wards whom they had fooled. Since the time of Gallienus at least, the churches as such had been officially allowed to possess property. Constantine laid down that any Roman citizen could at death leave gifts to the Church (XVI : 2 : 4). He had to justify this permission with an explanation. But the large-scale leaving of possessions to individual clerics and 'poor men', that is, to men who had officially renounced the world, to become 'monks', but who frequented society and hunted legacies, was a fairly new phenomenon. This was an age when some of the great western aristocrats were getting rid of their wealth on religious grounds. If the donor had been influenced by an individual, no doubt he would try to give him some. That the law is directed to the Eastern Prefect would indicate that in the east, too, rich people were thus giving away their wealth. The law legislates against the dishonest aggrandisement of charlatans, and no churchman should have objected.

Someone seems to have brought pressure to bear on the Emperor and he appears to have given in against his better judgment and the true welfare of the Church. The provisions about inheritance were abrogated by the next law in this section (XVI : 2 : 28).

The cult of the martyrs was widespread and abuses had crept in. Eunomius and Vigilantius opposed the cult but Theodosius, who was himself devoted to it (Sozomen, VII 21, tells us of his devotion to the Head of John the Baptist), tried to regulate it. He ordered that no one was to transfer a buried body to another place. He also forbade the dismembering of a martyr's body and the making of relic-mongering into a trade. Devotees were told they could venerate the martyr by building him a martyry and other buildings (IX : 17 : 7). Without doubt the Christian hierarchy would in their better moments have approved this law.

THEODOSIUS' LEGISLATION REGARDING THE JEWS[1]

Where the Jews came to be involved in the main stream of Theodosius' religious policy, his relationships with them have been discussed in the text. The purpose of this note is to enumerate and discuss briefly the laws regarding the Jews between 379 and 395.

detach women from their possessions! On shaving the head, see I Cor. 11.10, 15 and Gangra, Canon XVII. It is pathetic that the Emperor had nothing better to do than regulate female coiffure.

[1] On this subject in general see especially J. Juster, *Les Juifs dans l'empire romain*, 2 vols, Paris, 1914; F. Barth in *Theologische Zeitschrift aus der Schweiz*, 1889, pp. 65 ff. and M. Simon, *Verus Israel*, Paris, 1948. The writer is indebted to Rabbi Jacob Posen of the Nottingham synagogue for much instruction patiently given.

1. In April 383 by XII : 1 : 99, Gratian withdrew from the Jews those exemptions from curial burdens which had been granted them by law. The Emperor is probably referring to two laws of Constantine, XVI : 8 : 3 of 321 and XVI : 8 : 4 of 331 which exempted some Jews in every curial group and all synagogue servants. Gratian points out that Christian clergy do not enjoy these privileges.

2. In May 383, Gratian, in a law against Christians who turned to paganism and Manichaeism, included those who became Jews (XVI : 7 : 3). No punishment for those who became Jews is specified, though it is threatened. Apostasy to Judaism had been forbidden by the pre-Christian Emperors, and from Christianity to Judaism by Constantine and Constantius, so this was no new departure.[1]

3. In 384 (III : 1 : 5) Theodosius ordered that no Jew was to buy a Christian slave, or contaminate one who had come from Christianity with Jewish sacraments. If public investigation proved this had been done, the slaves were to be taken away by force and such masters were to undergo punishment suitable to the crime. In addition he ordered that if slaves, who were still Christian, or had been turned from Christians into Jews, were found in Jewish households, they were to be redeemed from unworthy servitude, a suitable price being paid by the Christians.

Eusebius says that Constantine forbade Jews to enslave any Christian (*Vit. Const.* IV 27). No law to this effect is preserved, but a law of 415 says that in accordance with the law of Constantine, if any Jew had a Christian slave, he was to be handed over to the Church (XVI : 8 : 22). Constantine also forbade Jews to buy and circumcise non-Jewish slaves. If they did, the slave was to be freed. The wording of the law (*mercatus circumciderit*) suggests that the prohibition was not on the buying, but on the circumcision (XVI : 9 : 1 of 335). Constantius went much further than his father. The purchase of non-Jewish slaves was forbidden. If the slave were circumcised, the culprit was to receive capital punishment. If a Jew bought Christians, they were to be confiscated (XVI : 9 : 2 of 339). In view of all this it may be said with confidence that in III : 1 : 5 Theodosius was treating the Jews more mildly than his Christian predecessors. Presumably a home-born Christian slave, or one bought in the past, remained with his Jewish master. Theodosius by this law did not contribute much to the policy by which the Jews were unable to possess non-Jewish slaves, a policy which is said to have driven them into commerce and usury.

4. Between 384 and 389 Theodosius ordered that *coloni* in Palestine

[1] Barth, *op. cit.*, p. 69; XVI : 8 : 1, cf. *Sirm.* IV and XVI : 8 : 7.

were to come under the same rules as *coloni* elsewhere. That is, pre-sumably, in contradiction to Jewish law, their serfdom was to be per-manent.[1] This law is no anti-Jewish measure but part of the process of standardization.

5. On 14 March 388 Theodosius ordered that no Jew was to receive a Christian woman in marriage, nor was a Christian to contract a union with a Jewess. A crime of this sort was to be the equivalent of adultery; the public was to be at liberty to make accusation (III : 7 : 2, repeated at IX : 7 : 5).

Constantius in 339 had ordered that women who had been employed in an imperial factory and had been led by the Jews into fellowship in their turpitude were to be returned to the factory.[2] For the future, the Jews were not to unite Christian women with their nefarious practices, and if they did, they involved themselves in danger of capital punishment. It is possible to suppose that this law forbade all marriages between Jews and Christian women, but this interpretation goes beyond the evidence, for the whole law may well be concerned only with women who were bound to some kind of imperial service in weaving or seraglio.

Even if Constantius by this law forbade Jewish men to marry Christian women, Theodosius was going beyond him in forbidding a Christian man to marry a Jewish woman. Theodosius' law put Jews and Christian on the same footing in the matter of mixed marriages. The Jews them-selves probably approved, in that since the days of Ezra and Nehemiah, they had disliked mixed marriages. Since this law was by no means a strongly anti-Jewish measure, there seems little justification for suggest-ing that it was laws like this which incited the people to anti-Jewish acts like burning the synagogue at Callinicum which took place later the same year (388).

6. In 390 the Emperor stated that the corporation of the Jews and Samaritans could not legally be called to serve as *navicularii* (that is, be responsible for the transport of goods, especially corn, to the capital). Individuals from among them who had the means could, however, be held liable for the duty (XIII : 5 : 18).

This law is so eminently just in its treatment of the Jews, that it has led some scholars to suppose that here Theodosius was being fair to them out of reaction away from Ambrose after the Callinicum affair. But if we

---

[1] *Cod. Just.*, XI : 51 : 1. On this law, see Pack, *Studies in Libanius*, p. 48; F. de Zulueta in Vinogradoff's *Oxford Studies in Social and Legal History*, I, Oxford, 1909, pp. 32 ff., and Juster, pp. 79 f.

[2] XVI : 8 : 6—'*quas Juadaei in turpitudinis suae duxere consortium*'; Juster, *op. cit.*, II, p. 47 says 'Il est évident que le terme *consortium* signifie marriage.'

accept the purport of his laws as outlined above, it would seem that he had been mild in his attitude to them all along, and this law is no great departure from his custom.

7. In 392 Theodosius upheld the right of the Jewish Patriarchs to eject unwanted members from their community (XVI : 8 : 8).[1] The Church insisted on this right in dealing with her own offenders,[2] so Theodosius is being only just to the Jews.

8. On 29 September 393 Theodosius sent a forthright law to Addeus, *comes et magister utriusque militiae per orientem*. It is clear enough that the sect of the Jews has been prohibited by no law. Wherefore the Emperor is gravely disturbed that in some places their meetings have been prevented. Therefore Addeus is, on the receipt of the order, to restrain with suitable severity the excess of those who, under the title of the Christian religion, engage in unlawful acts and try to destroy and pillage synagogues (XVI : 8 : 9).

This law in its clarity and directness may well reproduce the Emperor's very own words and sentiments. At a time when pagan shrines in many places had been pillaged by the Christians, Theodosius insists that the Jews are not to be submitted to the same treatment. St Ambrose and his ecclesiastical friends would have detested this law.

9. Another law of 393 by Theodosius dealing with the Jews appears in the *Codex Justinianus* (I : 9 : 7). It forbids the practice of polygamy among the Jews. It may be suggested that Theodosius is here, under Christian influence, interfering in the internal affairs of the Jews. Polygamy was by no means an integral part of Judaism, and the Jews as a body were not likely to resent this law or be much affected by it.

It may be said in conclusion that Theodosius throughout his reign maintained a friendly and just policy towards the Jews. Perhaps this was because he was a Roman and respected their ancient rights. Perhaps it was because in this matter he was a Christian of the tradition which goes back to St Paul, which believes that the Jews are a part of God's purpose in the world and a witness to his plan.

---

[1] The title '*clarissimus*' and '*illustris*' used in this law of the Jewish patriarch were used of people with the rank of Praetorian Prefect. We do not know when the patriarchs were given this honour. Seeck, *Gesch.* V 226 suggests it was given soon after the Callinicum affair, but though this is possible, there is no evidence for this dating. T. Klauser, *Der Ursprung der bischöflichen Insignien und Ehrenrechte*, Krefeld, 1949, takes it that the more important bishops had this rank at the time because the Jewish patriarch has it. He does not attempt to date the granting of the privilege. XVI : 8 : 22 of 415 mentions that Gamaliel had been made an honorary Prefect.

[2] Nicaea, Canon V; Constantinople, Canon VI (382).

E

The Coins[1]

OUR NUMISMATIC guides have rightly emphasized the importance of coins for instructional purposes in a state where many people are illiterate.[2] One would have expected much from an Emperor like Theodosius who has a great reputation for spreading Christianity. Alas, after much study where one has followed a number of likely clues, one can only bring forward some rather unimpressive scraps.

THE USE OF THE LABARUM ON THE COINS

The labarum is frequently found in the Emperor's hand in conjunction with such reverse legends as *'restitutor reipublicae'*, *'triumfator gent. barb.'*, *'spes reipublicae'*, *'securitas reipublicae'*, *'virtus exercitus'*. It is possible that the libarum only suggested to the beholder the battlefield and the great days of Constantine. On the other hand it may have linked the success and welfare of the commonwealth with the Emperor's dependence on the God of the Christians. Also the coins reflect the actual military ensigns in use and presumably pagan soldiers too had to reverence this emblem associated with Christianity. The labarum more often than not was inserted into an antecedent design and while it did not too ostentatiously advertise Christianity, it played some part in proclaiming the Christianity of the Emperors.

THE COINS OF FLACCILLA AND THE 'SALUS REIPUBLICAE' TYPES

It is probable that no coin was struck for Flaccilla at a mint outside Theodosius' direct control. Her coins date from her becoming Augusta in 383, to her death in 386. Her obverses are of the same type, 'AEL FLAC-CILLA AVG, Empress' bust draped, with elaborate head-dress, necklace and mantle'. The reverses are of three kinds:

(*i*) 'SALVS REI-PVBLICAE. Victory seated r. writing *chi rho* on shield resting on small column.'

[1] The writer is greatly indebted to the kindness and ready help of the late J. W. E. Pearce, and the staff of the Coin Rooms at the British and Ashmolean Museums.

[2] For the idea itself clearly set forth see: M. Grant, *Roman History from Coins*, Cambridge, 1958, chapter 1. Cf. the fine African coin series showing the head of Dr Kwame Nkrumah with the words CONDITOR CIVITATIS GHANIENSIS. At the time of issue it was stated that these coins would make it plain to everyone that rule was no longer in foreign hands.

(*ii*) 'SALVS REI-PVBLICAE. Empress standing facing, head r., with arms folded on breast.' It is possible that the Empress is in a gesture of prayer, as if to suggest that the safety of the state depends on this.

(*iii*) '*Chi rho* in wreath' covers the entire reverse.

It would seem then that the coins of Flaccilla, though few in number, frequently bring Christianity into prominence. Possibly this was because Flaccilla chose the types for herself; in this case they represent her own views, but we know that she had great influence on her husband. On the other hand, the types may have been chosen by Theodosius himself and represent his views. If this is so, perhaps he felt freer to express his Christianity in coins which were not as highly official, sacred, and common as his own.

After Flaccilla's death, Theodosius seems to have continued to connect Christian symbolism with the '*Salus Reipublicae*'. At least it can be said that after 388 Theodosian mints began to issue a type of *Aes* IV (a very common coin) bearing the reverse legend 'SALVS REI-PVBLICAE', showing 'victory advancing, with left hand dragging captive, carrying trophy over right shoulder. In left field *chi rho*.' This coin was issued by the mints of Constantinople and Cyzicus.[1] At Nicomedia, Antioch and Alexandria the same coin appears but the *chi rho* is in the mint-mark.[2] Theodosius appears to have brought the type with him to the west, for in the period 388–93 it begins to appear at Aquileia, Rome and Thessalonica.[3] Valentinian II does not seem to have followed suit, for the coin does not appear at Lugdunum and Arelate, but it is not possible to build much on this, in that neither Mediolanum, Siscia, Sirmium nor Heraclea show the coin.

Here perhaps we have a definite indication in the coins of Theodosius' increased Christian zeal. Of course the coins do not indicate exactly when this came—it was, so far as numismatic evidence can tell us, some time between 388 and 392. On the other hand, not very much stress can be laid on the appearance of a small *chi rho* on the coins. It had appeared regularly and fairly commonly since the days of Constantine.

THE 'VOTA' COINS

Theodosius issued *vota* coins in the normal way in the early years of his reign, though he seems to have used the numbering of his *Aes* IV

---

[1] Pearce, pp. 234, 236, 246 f.

[2] Pearce, pp. 262 f., 291, 303 f. At Antioch Flaccilla's reverse, '*Salus Reipublicae* with victory writing *chi rho* on shield', appears with Theodosius in the obverse.

[3] Pearce, pp. 106 f., 133, 136, 188.

eastern coinage as a means of expressing a seniority in the purple which was not really his.[1]

The issues of 379 and 383–4 are known to us. There was also a *vota publica* issue which is dated by Pearce to the period 388–92 (p. 81). This seems a likely dating, for *vota publica* coins of exactly the same type were issued at Milan for both Theodosius and Valentinian II, and a time soon after their defeat of Maximus would be most appropriate. H. Mattingly, senior, however, wishes to date this coin to 383, apparently because there would be 'a slight inconsistency between the celebration of these special vows and the omission of the normal numbered issues'.[2] One cannot disagree with an expert, but on the whole, at this point, Pearce seems to be correct. Mattingly points out that the two *vota* first mentioned are 'the last numbered vows of Theodosius I, though he lived long enough to celebrate his "*vota XV multa XX*" and his "*vota XX multa XXX*". The absence of the later celebrations surely reflects the aversion of a strictly orthodox Christian Emperor to the paganism that still clung to the vows.' He points out that Valentinian II celebrated his later vows, 'but we have to remember that he was based on Rome, with its still obstinate paganism'.

We have tried to show above that just at the time when he was failing, so Mattingly would suggest, to celebrate *vota XV multa XX*, Theodosius was showing favour to pagans, even courting their support, and that Valentinian II was not based on Rome, but relegated to Gaul. It would have been more to the point had Mattingly referred to the *vota* of Arcadius and Honorius, who were under Theodosius' control. He himself shows that Honorius took the vows in 393, and Arcadius probably in 387–8.[3]

The word '*vota*' in connection with the official vows of the Emperors does not occur in the Code, but the Code at least indicates that Theodosius permitted *vota* customs at the New Year.[4] At VII : 24 : 1 of 5 March 395 Honorius mentions offerings of gold connected with the *vota* at the New Year as if these were the custom. This law comes so soon after his father's death that it may be taken as evidence for the custom during the later years of his reign. It is impossible to argue from silence that because numbered *vota* coins for the second half of his reign do not survive, he neglected the *vota* celebrations on religious grounds.

[1] J. W. E. Pearce, 'The *Vota* legends on the Roman coinage', *Num. Chron.*, 5th series, XVII, 1937, pp. 112–23; *Roman Imperial Coinage* IX, p. vi.
[2] H. Mattingly, 'The Imperial *Vota*', *Proceedings of the British Academy* XXXVI, pp. 244 f., 263.
[3] *Op. cit.*, pp. 246, 250. *Vota* issues in both west and east continued till late into the fifth century.
[4] XVI : 10 : 8 of 382.

We may now ask what were, in brief, the theological implications of Christian Emperors celebrating the vows. They were in essence good-luck ceremonies seeking to enlist superhuman powers on the side of the Emperor. The ceremony seems to have been in basis magical as much as religious.[1] Therefore, when the Emperor became a Christian, it was possible for him to omit the incense, libations and bloody sacrifices, or to appoint a deputy. The Church grew restive about the custom, but the first conciliar action in the east against the *vota* was not taken till the Council in Trullo, 692. The imperial *vota* had by this time died out. Theodosius may be said, then, to have countenanced these ceremonies which were, if not pagan, certainly sub-Christian, but in this he did not differ from his fellows.

We have given above what appear to be outstanding examples of Christian themes, and an example of what at first sight appeared to be a remnant of paganism. The most important conclusion one can draw from a study of Theodosius' coins is a 'positive negative'.[2] It means a good deal that we can find nothing that is unequivocally and outspokenly pagan on the coins of Theodosius. It is also rather surprising that this most Christian Emperor has so little that is strikingly Christian on his coins. It is true that Constantine, once he became convincedly Christian, dropped many pagan motives and others were gradually eliminated, but some lingered on till Valens. Christian motives only came in gradually. Constantine introduced the *chi rho* and labarum. Nonetheless, between Constantine and Theodosius there are some coins which have a definitely Christian intent. For instance, there is the type which bears a large *alpha, chi-rho, omega* on the reverse.[3] This coin connects the *Salus* of the rulers with Christianity. Then there is a Vetranio and a Constantius II reverse showing the Emperor being crowned by a Victory who is behind him. He is holding a labarum. The legend is: HOC SIGNO VICTOR ERIS.[4]

Another remarkable coin is an *Aes* III issued by Valentinian I at Sirmium during 364. The reverse legend is PERPETVIT-AS IMPERII. The Emperor, standing, is receiving a shield from a hand above. On the shield is a swastika. J. W. E. Pearce (p. 156) says of it: 'This unique *Aes* III with its definitely Christian symbolism may be a trial piece suppressed

---

[1] G. Wissowa, *Religion und Kultus der Römer*, 2nd ed., Munich, 1912, pp. 381 ff.; F. Kenner, *Num. Zeit.* (Vienna) XII, 1880, pp. 74 ff. See also Alföldi, *A Festival of Isis*, pp. 42 ff.

[2] The phrase is one used by Dr C. H. V. Sutherland.

[3] Magnentius: Cohen VIII, p. 13; Decentius: p. 25.

[4] Cohen VIII, p. 4; VII, p. 461.

at this stage by the danger of antagonizing pagan sentiment at the out-
set of the new reign. If the symbolism is definitely Christian, it is significant that the coin was not brought into common use.'

It is disappointing to record that Theodosius' numismatic policy in
matters religious was much the same as that of his predecessors and colleagues, including those who were Arian in tendency. It is difficult to
find an explanation. Perhaps Theodosius did not want to proclaim his
Christianity, in that before the Battle of the Frigidus paganism was still
very strong. He was content to fulminate in the laws against paganism,
but the laws would be seen only by a select few, while the coins entered
every household. Perhaps, once the pagan gods were eliminated and
before Christ was brought in, the Emperor enjoyed being the focus of
numismatic attention. Perhaps in an innately conservative and fossilizing
society it was easier to stop in the ease of ambivalent motives than to
introduce something new.

BIBLIOGRAPHY

ALFÖLDI, A. *The Conversion of Constantine and Pagan Rome*, Oxford, 1948.
— *A Conflict of Ideas in the Late Roman Empire*, Oxford, 1952.
ALLARD, P. *Le Christianisme et l'Empire Romain de Néron à Théodose*, 3rd ed., Paris, 1903.
BARDY, G. *L'église et les derniers Romains*, Paris, 1948.
BATIFFOL, P. *La paix constantinienne et le catholicisme*, Paris, 1914.
— *Le siège apostolique, 359–451*, Paris, 1924.
BAUR, C. *Der hl. Chrysostomus und seine Zeit*, 2 vols, Munich, 1929/30.
BAYNES, N. H. *Constantine the Great and the Christian Church* (Raleigh Lecture), London, 1926.
— *The 'Historia Augusta', its date and purpose*, Oxford, 1926.
BESSELL, W. *Über das Leben des Ulfilas*, Göttingen, 1860.
BOISSIER, G. *La fin du paganisme*, 2 vols, Paris, 1891.
BOYD, W. K. *The Ecclesiastical Edicts of the Theodosian Code*, New York, 1905.
BRAUN, O. 'Syrische Texte über die erste allgemeine Synode von Konstantinopel', *Orientalische Studien Theodor Nöldeke zum siebzigsten Geburtstag gewidmet*, ed. Carl Bezold, vol. I, pp. 463–78, Gieszen, 1906.
BRIGHT, W. *The Canons of the First Four General Councils*, Oxford, 1892.
BURKITT, F. C. *The Religion of the Manichees*, Cambridge, 1925.
CAMPENHAUSEN, H. VON. *Ambrosius von Mailand als Kirchenpolitiker*, Berlin, 1929.
CASPAR, E. *Geschichte des Papsttums von den Anfängen bis zur Höhe der Weltherrschaft*, vol. I: *Römische Kirche und Imperium Romanum*, Tübingen, 1930.
CAVALLERA, F. *Le Schisme d'Antioche*, Paris, 1905.
CERNJAVSKIJ, N. *Feodosij Veliky i ego religioznaja politika*, St Petersburg, 1913 (not seen).
CHALMERS, W. 'The NEA EKDOSIS of Eunapius' Histories', *The Classical Quarterly*, N.S. III, 1953, pp. 165–70.
COCHRANE, C. N. *Christianity and Classical Culture*, Oxford, 1940.
COHEN, H. *Description des monnaies frappées sous l'Empire Romain* (esp. vol. VIII), Paris, 1880 ff.
CUMONT, F. *Les religions orientales*, Paris, 1929.
DEVREESSE, R. *Le Patriarcat d'Antioche*, Paris, 1945.
DILL, S. *Roman Society in the Last Century of the Western Empire*, 2nd ed., London, 1925.
DÖLGER, F. J. *Antike und Christentum*, 6 vols, Münster, 1929 ff.
DOWNEY, G. 'Themistius and the Defense of Hellenism in the Fourth Century', *HTR* L, 1957, pp. 259–74.
DUCHESNE, L. *Histoire ancienne de l'église*, vols. II (4th ed.) and III (3rd ed.), Paris, 1910.

DUDDEN, F. HOMES. *The Life and Times of St Ambrose*, 2 vols, Oxford, 1935.
EGGER, R. 'Der erste Theodosius', *Byzantion* V, 1930.
ELLIS, R. 'On a recently discovered Latin poem of the 4th Century', *Journal of Philology* I, 1868, pp. 66–80.
ENSSLIN, W. *Die Religionspolitik des Kaisers Theodosius der Grosse* (Sitzungsberichte der Bayerischen Akademie der Wissenschaften, phil.-hist. Kl., 1953, *Heft* 2), Munich, 1953.
— 'Staat und Kirche von Konstantin bis Theodosius', *Acts of the Second International Byzantine Congress*, Athens, 1956, pp. 404–15.
FESTUGIÈRE, A. J. *Antioche païenne et chrétienne*, Paris, 1959.
FLÉCHIER, V. *Histoire de Théodose le Grand*, Paris, 1681.
FUNK, F. X. 'Die Berufung der ökumenischen Synoden des Altertums', *Kirchengeschichtliche Abhandlungen und Untersuchungen*, vol. I, pp. 39–86.
— 'Zur Frage nach der Berufung, der allgemeinen Synoden des Altertums', *ibid.* III, pp. 143–9, 406–39.
GEFFCKEN, J. *Der Ausgang des griechisch-römischen Heidentums*, 2nd ed., Heidelberg, 1929.
GEPPERT, F. *Die Quellen des Kirchenhistorikers Socrates Scholasticus*, Leipzig, 1898.
GERLAND, E. 'Die Vorgeschichte des Patriarchates von Konstantinopel', *Byzantinisch-neugriechische Jahrbücher*, 1932, pp. 217–30.
GIBBON, E. *The History of the Decline and Fall of the Roman Empire*, ed. J. B. Bury, 7 vols, London, 1897.
GLAESENER, H. 'L'Empereur Gratien et S. Ambroise', *Revue d'histoire ecclesiastique* LII, 1957, pp. 466 ff.
GOEBEL, R. *De Ioannis Chrysostomi et Libanii orationibus quae sunt de seditione Antiochensium*, Göttingen, 1910.
GOTHOFREDUS, J. *Codex Theodosianus cum perpetuis commentariis*, Lyons, 1665.
— *Idem*, ed. J. D. Ritter, Leipzig, 1736–1745.
GRADENWITZ, O. *Heidelberger Index zum Theodosianus*, Berlin, 1929.
GRANT, M. *Roman Anniversary Issues. An exploratory study of the numismatic and medallic commemoration of anniversary years 49 B.C.–375 A.D.* Cambridge, 1950.
GREENSLADE, S. L. 'The Illyrican Churches and the Vicariate of Thessalonica 378–95', *JTS* XLVI, 1945, pp. 17 ff.
— *Schism in the Early Church*, London, 1953.
— *Church and State from Constantine to Theodosius*, London, 1954.
GRÉGOIRE, H. 'Le préfet du prétoire Fl. Eutolmius Tatianus' in *Anatolian Studies presented to Sir William Ramsay*, ed. W. Buckler and W. Calder, Manchester, 1923, pp. 151 ff.
GRINDA, F. *Der Panegyricus des Pakatus*, Strassburg, 1916.
GÜLDENPENNING, A. *Die Kirchengeschichte des Theodoret von Kyrrhos*, Halle, 1889.
GÜLDENPENNING, A. and IFLAND, J. *Der Kaiser Theodosius der Grosse*, Halle, 1878.
GWATKIN, H. M. *Studies of Arianism*, 2nd ed., Cambridge, 1900.

HASSE, F. *Altchristliche Kirchengeschichte nach orientalischen Quellen*, Leipzig, 1927.

HARTKE, W. *Römische Kinderkaiser*, Berlin, 1951.

HEFELE, C. J. and LECLERCQ, H. *Histoire des conciles d'après les documents originaux*, Paris, 1907 ff.

HODGKIN, T. *The Dynasty of Theodosius*, Oxford, 1889.

HONIGMANN, E. 'Recherches sur les listes des Pères de Nicée et de Constantinople', *Byzantion* XI 2, 1936, pp. 440 ff.

HOWARD, G. B. *The canons of the primitive Church together with the creeds of Nicaea and Constantinople. Trans. from Br. Mus. MS 14,528*, London, 1896.

HUTTMAN, M. A. *The establishment of Christianity and the proscription of Paganism*, New York, 1914.

JALLAND, T. *The Church and the Papacy*, London, 1944.

JEEP, L. 'Quellenuntersuchungen zu den griechischen Kirchenhistori-kern', *Jahrbücher für klassische Philologie*, suppl. Band XIV, Leipzig, 1885, pp. 53–178.

JUSTER, J. *Les Juifs dans l'Empire Romain*, 2 vols, Paris, 1914.

KANIECKA, M. S. *Vita S. Ambrosii a Paulino* (Catholic University of America Patristic Studies 16), Washington, 1928.

KAUFFMANN, F. *Aus der Schule des Wulfila*, Strassburg, 1899.

KELLY, J. N. D. *Early Christian Creeds*, London, 1950.

— *Early Christian Doctrines*, London, 1958.

KELLY, T. A. *Sancti Ambrosii liber de consolatione Valentiniani* (Catholic University of America Patristic Studies 58), Washington, 1940.

LABRIOLLE, P. DE. *La réaction paienne*, Paris, 1934.

LIETZMANN, H. *From Constantine to Julian*, London, 1950; *The Era of the Church Fathers*, 1951, being vols 3 and 4 of the translation of his *Geschichte der alten Kirche*.

MANNIX, M. D. *S. Ambrosii de obitu Theodosii* (Catholic University of America Patristic Studies 9), Washington, 1925. (Cf. also *CSEL* LXXIII.)

MARTROYE, F. 'La répression de la magie et le culte des gentils au IVe siecle', *Revue historique de droit français et étranger*, 4e serie IX, 1930, pp. 669 ff.

OLIVIER, N. *De Theodosii Magni constitutionibus*, Diss., Lugduni Batavorum, 1835.

ORTROY, F. VAN. 'Saint Ambroise et l'empereur Théodose', *Analecta Bollandiana* XXIII, 1904, pp. 417–26.

OULTON, J. E. L. 'Rufinus' translation of the Church History of Eusebius', *JTS* XXX, 1929, pp. 150 ff.

PACK, R. A. *Studies in Libanius and Antiochene Society under Theodosius*, Diss., Michigan, 1935.

PALANQUE, J. R., BARDY, G., LABRIOLLE, P. DE. *De la paix constantinienne a la mort de Théodose* (Fliche et Martin, *Histoire de l'église* III), Paris, 1947.

PALANQUE, J. R. S. *Ambroise et l'Empire Romain*, Paris, 1933.

— *Essai sur la préfecture du prétoire du Bas-Empire*, Paris, 1933.

PEARCE, J. W. E. *Valentinian I–Theodosius I* (vol. IX of *The Roman Imperial Coinage*), London, 1951.

PETIT, P. *Libanius et la vie municipale à Antioche au IVe siècle*, Paris, 1955.

— *Les Étudiants de Libanius*, Paris, 1957.

PHARR, C. *The Theodosian Code, the Novels and the Sirmondian Constitutions. A translation*, Princeton, 1952.

PIGANIOL, A. *L'Empire chrétien*, Paris, 1947.

RAUSCHEN, G. *Jahrbücher der christlichen Kirche unter dem Kaiser Theodosius dem Grossen*, Freiburg, 1897.

SCHOO, G. *Die Quellen des Kirchenhistorikers Sozomenos*, Berlin, 1911.

SCHULTHESS, F. 'Die syrischen Kanones der Synoden von Nicaea bis Chalcedon', *Abhandlungen der königlichen Gesellschaft der Wissenschaften zu Göttingen*, phil.-hist. Kl., N.F., X 2, Berlin, 1908.

SCHWARTZ, E. *Acta conciliorum oecumenicorum*, Strassburg, 1914 ff.

— 'Uber die Bischofslisten der Synoden von Chalkedon, Nicaea, und Konstantinopel', *Abhandlungen der Bayerischen Akademie der Wissenschaften, phil.-hist. Abt.*, N.F., Heft 13, 1937.

— 'Die Kanonessammlungen der alten Reichskirche', *Zeitschrift der Savigny-Stiftung* LVI, *kanon. Abt.* XXV, 1936, pp. 1–114.

— 'Zur Kirchengeschichte des vierten Jahrhunderts', *ZNTW* XXXIV, 1935, pp. 129–213.

— 'Über Kirchengeschichte', *Gesammelte Schriften* I, pp. 116 ff., Berlin, 1938.

— 'Die Konzilien des 4 und 5 Jahrhunderts', *Historische Zeitschrift*, CIV, 1910, pp. 1–37.

— 'Das Nicaenum und das Constantinopolitanum auf der Synode von Chalkedon', *ZNTW* XXV, 1926, pp. 38 ff.

— 'Reichskonzilien von Theodosius bis Justinian', *ZS-S* XLII, *kanon. Abt.* XI, 1921, pp. 208–53.

— 'Über die Sammlung des Codex Veronensis LX', *ZNTW* XXXV, 1936, pp. 1–23.

SEECK, O. *Geschichte des Untergangs der antiken Welt*, 6 vols, Berlin and Stuttgart, 1909–1921.

— *Regesten der Kaiser und Päpste für die Jahre 311 bis 476 n. Chr.*, Stuttgart, 1919.

STEIN, E. *Geschichte des spätrömischen Reiches. I–Vom römischen zum byzantinischen Staate* (284–476 n. Chr.), Vienna, 1928.

STUFFKEN, J. H. *Dissertatio de Theodosii Magni in rem Christianam Meritis*, Lugduni Batavorum, 1828.

THOMPSON, E. A. *The Historical Work of Ammianus Marcellinus*, Cambridge, 1947.

TILLEMONT, LENAIN DE. *Histoire des empereurs*, vols IV and V, Paris, 1697 and 1701.

— *Mémoires pour servir à l'histoire ecclésiastique*, vols IV ff., Paris, 1696.

TURNER, C. H. *Ecclesiae occidentalis monumenta iuris antiquissima*, Oxford, 1899 ff.

WYTZES, J. *Der Streit um den Altar der Victoria*, Amsterdam, 1936.

ZEILLER, J. *L'Empire Romain et l'église*, Paris, 1938

I. INDEX OF NAMES

I

II. INDEX OF SUBJECTS

III. INDEX TO LAWS CITED FROM CODEX THEODOSIANUS

II: 8: 1, 18 108
II: 8: 19 67, 108f., 110
II: 8: 21 100

III: 1: 5 116
III: 7: 2 117
III: 8: 1 54

IV: 22: 3 66

VI: 27: 6 103

VII: 24: 1 121

VIII: 4: 16 59
VIII: 8: 1 108

IX: 7: 3 68
IX: 7: 5 117
IX: 7: 6 68, 102
IX: 16: 7–9 19
IX: 16: 11 73
IX: 17: 7 115
IX: 35: 4 109
IX: 35: 5 110
IX: 38: 2–4 109
IX: 38: 6 60, 109
IX: 38: 7f. 73, 109
IX: 40: 13 103
IX: 40: 15 113
IX: 44: 1 60
IX: 45: 1 114

X: 1: 8 73
X: 1: 12 72
X: 3: 4 73

XI: 7: 13 108
XI: 16: 18 103

XI: 20: 6 73
XI: 36: 31 113
XI: 39: 8, 10 113

XII: 1: 49f., 59, 99, 104, 112 111
XII: 1: 121, 123 112

XIII: 5: 18 117
XIII: 5: 19 103

XV: 5: 2 108
XV: 14: 6–8 63

XVI: 1: 2 28ff., 51
XVI: 1: 3 44ff.
XVI: 1: 4 55ff.
XVI: 2: 3 111
XVI: 2: 4 115
XVI: 2: 19 111
XVI: 2: 20 114f.
XVI: 2: 25 28
XVI: 2: 26 113
XVI: 2: 27 114f.
XVI: 2: 28 103, 115
XVI: 3: 1 65, 103
XVI: 3: 2 65
XVI: 4: 1 56f.
XVI: 4: 2 62
XVI: 5: 3 51
XVI: 5: 4 23
XVI: 5: 5 23f.
XVI: 5: 6 23, 34ff., 41
XVI: 5: 7 51f.
XVI: 5: 9 51
XVI: 5: 11 41, 51, 54

XVI: 5: 12 41, 54
XVI: 5: 13 54
XVI: 5: 14 47, 57
XVI: 5: 15, 17 58
XVI: 5: 20 51
XVI: 5: 21f. 59
XVI: 5: 23 58
XVI: 5: 25 58f.
XVI: 5: 27 58
XVI: 5: 29 59
XVI: 5: 65 41
XVI: 7: 1f. 52
XVI: 7: 3 51f., 116
XVI: 7: 4f. 52
XVI: 8: 1, 3 f. 116
XVI: 8: 6 117
XVI: 8: 7 116
XVI: 8: 8 66, 118
XVI: 8: 9 118
XVI: 8: 22 66, 116, 118
XVI: 9: 1f. 116
XVI: 10: 7 73
XVI: 10: 8 72
XVI: 10: 9 73
XVI: 10: 10 78, 105
XVI: 10: 11 78f., 104f.
XVI: 10: 12 84f.
XVI: 10: 13 86
XVI: 10: 20 21, 73

Sirmondianae

III 111
IV 116
VII 109
VIII 110

18046